THE PRIVATE OFFICE REVISITED

The Private Office 2001.

NICHOLAS HENDERSON

THE PRIVATE OFFICE
REVISITED

*A personal account of life in the Private Office of five
Secretaries of State for Foreign Affairs, and an inside view of
that office and of subsequent Ministers seen in recent times.*

PROFILE BOOKS

First published in Great Britain in 2001 by
Profile Books Ltd
58A Hatton Garden
London ECIN 8LX
www.profilebooks.co.uk

10 9 8 7 6 5 4 3 2 1

Typeset in Minion by MacGuru
info@macguru.org.uk

Printed and bound in Great Britain by
St Edmundsbury Press, Bury St Edmunds

A CIP catalogue record for this book is available from the British Library.

ISBN 1 86197 500 7

To the memory of Bob Dixon

CONTENTS

ILLUSTRATIONS

The photograph reproduced on the endpapers (by Derry
   Moore) shows the Foreign Secretary's room in 2001. Note the
   bust of Ernest Bevin.

ACKNOWLEDGEMENTS

My gratitude goes to those who served with me in the Private Office in the two terms I was there: Bob Dixon, Nicholas Lawford, Guy Millard, John Henniker-Major, Pat Kinna, Jeremy Thomas, Norman Young, Irene Easton, Tom Bridges, Nicholas Fenn, Roger James and Jean Elliott.

I was helped over my original book by Jock Colville, Ian Gilmour, Roy Jenkins, Ferdinand Mount, George Walden and Bobbie de Margerie.

Margaret Chester has given me invaluable editorial advice over this new edition, in which I have also been helped by Len Appleyard, Sherard Cowper-Coles, William Ehrman, Brian Fall, John Grant, Peter Hennessy, John Kerr and Stephen Wall.

PROLOGUE

Nearly twenty years ago I wrote a book on the subject of the Private Office[1], giving personal details of my time with five Foreign Ministers, emphasizing the importance of the office and the high responsibility in government of the relatively young group of people in that Private Office and in the other private offices in Whitehall. I concluded with some generalizations about the nature of *homo politicus* as seen from a nearby range.

The book is now out of print. To meet a continuing demand, noticeably from those who want a view from inside of how one part of the government works, a picture based more on personal evidence rather than institutional analysis, Profile Books have decided to publish this new edition. Except for a few typographical

---

1 *The Private Office, A personal view of five Foreign Secretaries and of government from the inside*, Weidenfeld and Nicolson, 1984. The use of the term, Private Office, throughout Whitehall is comparatively recent. It became general in World War II, thanks to Winston Churchill, who had been accustomed to it at the Admiralty where it had been employed for a long time. Before that, people in the Foreign Office spoke of going to see the Private Secretary, not the Private Office.

or grammatical corrections, it contains the verbatim text of the earlier version, with this Prologue in place of the former Preface.

I have also added an Epilogue in which I have tried to show, on the basis of information from subsequent private secretaries, how far the role of their office has changed in the intervening years and whether, from their equally close standpoint, they have any different perspective from mine about the distinctive character of politicians, and their relationship with officials.

The daily lives of the private secretaries, like those of the Secretary of State himself and many of the officials in the Department, have been profoundly changed in recent times by the intensification of media coverage of foreign affairs. Any surprising event, any drama and particularly any tragedy anywhere in the world soon becomes a matter of global interest and often of concern. A reaction is almost invariably called for from the Foreign and Commonwealth Office (FCO) – and quickly. It might well be argued that there is no need to react to every crisis and that only matters of direct concern to British interests or lives should require an official response. Perhaps we in this country are too ready to become involved, and maybe this flows from the sense we have – however subconsciously – that we are still a global power. But while we no longer have that role militarily, I think that the British people do retain some humanitarian feeling of far-reaching responsibility, which can best be summed up in the Latin tag of Terence: '*Homo sum; humani nil a me alienum puto.*'[2]

A major modification in the character of private offices

---

2 'I am a man; I count nothing human foreign to me.'

compared with a generation ago, has been the increase in the number of political appointees. The first of the kind in the FCO arrived in 1964 during my time in the Private Office, when Labour had just come to power under Harold Wilson. John Harris,[3] who had been personal assistant to Hugh Gaitskell when the latter was Leader of the Opposition, became special assistant to the Foreign Secretary. The idea has caught on and been followed with enthusiasm by politicians of both parties, with the result that by mid-2001 there were some sixty 'special advisers to Ministers', as the *Civil Service Year Book* designated them. In Blair's first government Robin Cook, the Foreign Secretary, had two 'special advisers'. Others were brought in from time to time. Jack Straw has appointed two. These political appointees may not strictly be regarded as belonging to the established idea of the Private Office of a Minister, but in practice differentiation between their roles and those of the civil servants has become increasingly blurred, as I will illustrate later, and what matters is that they add to the importance of the Minister's Office as such – of which the traditional Private Office is the nucleus[4]. Currently there are seventy-eight special advisors to Ministers, of whom twenty-six

---

3 John Harris, later Baron Harris of Greenwich, 1930–2001.

4 After Blair first became Prime Minister he wanted to make Jonathan Powell, formerly but no longer a civil servant, his Principal Private Secretary at No. 10, but the Secretary of the Cabinet, Sir Robin Butler, strongly objected. This had always been a civil service post and there were good reasons why it should continue to be. The Principal Private Secretary has responsibilities that have to be kept out of politics, such as relations with the rest of Whitehall, including the Security Service and dealings with the honours system. Mr Blair did not appear to acknowledge the validity of the distinction. The outcome was a draw: a civil servant succeeded as Principal Private Secretary, but Powell became head of the Prime Minister's Office, with the title of 'Chief of Staff'.

are at No. 10. At the end of Mrs Thatcher's time there were eighteen at No. 10. So controversial has been the creeping politicisation of Whitehall and its possible constitutional implications that a special enquiry on the subject by the Committee on Standards and Public Life under Sir Nigel Wicks has been commissioned.

Under Blair 2, the Prime Minister's Office has become more extensive numerically and geographically. Posts have been duplicated for advice on foreign policy, and triplicated for public relations and contacts with the Labour Party, the aim being to achieve more effective 'delivery' – new-speak devised by ex new-Labour. Needless to say, No. 10 is not large enough to accomodate them all. Some will move into the Cabinet Office. The line between civil servants and political advisers will become even more blurred than hitherto thanks to the suggestion made that some of the new team will be regarded as having 'dual nationality'. The comparison that may be drawn with the White House does not do justice to the control the PM and his 'deliverers' will have, backed as they now are by an overwhelming majority in the House of Commons, compared with the limitation imposed on the authority of the President and his staff by the Congress and the division of powers in the USA Constitution.

Until my book was published I do not think that much comprehensive historical, constitutional or public attention had been given to the role of the Private Office in the decision-making process of British foreign policy. In his book, *Inside The Foreign Office*[5], published ten years ago, John Dickie, who had been

---

5 John Dickie, *Inside The Foreign Office*, Chapman, 1992, p.70.

Diplomatic Correspondent of the *Daily Mail* for thirty years, wrote that in all the many enquiries over the years into how the Foreign Office could be better run, the Private Office of foreign secretaries has been carefully shielded from prying eyes. He did some successful prying himself and concluded that this 'power house of the Foreign Office' had remained unchanged from 1945 when Ernest Bevin first found it, 'because it can get things done as no other part of the system can'.

The Franks Report on the Falkland Islands conflict of 1982[6] provided an instance of the inattention paid to the role of the Private Office in the analysis of decisions on foreign policy. Ten members of the Foreign and Commonwealth Office gave evidence to the Franks Committee, but none were from the Private Office.

More recently a few instances have occurred in which the participation of the Private Office has been brought to light (for example, in the Sandline saga, the Scott enquiry and the Hinduja affair). But the Private Office is not a customary hunting ground for those ferreting out the source of some disputed decision. This may not be so surprising if it is borne in mind that the chart of the organization of the Foreign and Commonwealth Office given in the latest *Civil Service Year Book* lists twenty-one departments of the office but makes no reference to the existence of the Private Office.

From the standpoint of day-to-day policy I do not think that the widespread ignorance of the role of the Private Office

---

6 *Falkland Islands Review: Report of a Committee of Privy Counsellors, Chairman, The Rt.Hon. the Lord Franks, January 1983, Cmnd.8787.*

matters. On the contrary, I think it is better that way, as I shall explain later. But historians can have reason to complain that it is sometimes difficult to determine the rationale for some foreign policy decision because notes by the Private Secretary, often attached to papers on submission to the Minister, perhaps in the overnight box, have been removed when the file is returned to the department. This may sound a devious practice but it corresponds to the requirement of the Secretary of State to have the benefit of the views of the Private Secretary, given his personal knowledge of ministerial objectives, while safeguarding the needs of the Private Secretary for discretion and the avoidance of any impression that he is usurping the function of one or other political department.

In my original book I explained that no hard and fast time is set for service in a Private Office; it can be anything between, say, two and five years. No particular qualifications are required for appointment to a Private Office, though obviously some people will be more temperamentally suited to it than others. No training or prior instruction is provided for the post; you are meant to adapt to it, and pick it up as you go along, a feature of the British system of government that I think is unique and valuable, even if it is no doubt regarded by some as another example of its unprofessionalism. Many of those who later attain high positions in the Diplomatic Service or in a home department will have served in a Private Office at one time or another in their career; and the years they have spent near the sun are bound to be among their most formative and indelible experiences.

From talking to former Foreign Ministers and reading their memoirs I have been left in no doubt about the importance to them of their Private Offices, both personally and for the conduct of public business. For contrasted reasons neither ministers nor private secretaries have been disposed to say publicly how crucial to government the post is and how delicate the relationship. As pointed out by Sir Percy Cradock, a long-time observer of the Whitehall scene and foreign policy adviser to Mrs Thatcher at No 10, this may be because ministers 'prefer to keep the memoirs field to themselves, expecting their advisers (civil servants) to maintain a respectful silence'. Cradock adds that 'most officials are content to leave it so'.[7] Despite the greater openness of modern government, I suspect that they are likely to continue to nourish 'a passion for anonymity', a phrase, as I record later, used about Tom Jones, the renowned member of Lloyd George's secretariat in World War I, but still apparently applicable to most of those who have worked in a private office in recent times.

---

7 Sir Percy Cradock, *In Pursuit of British Interests*, John Murray, 1997, p.2.

1

THE ROLE OF PRIVATE SECRETARY

The Private Secretaries to Ministers are the impresarios of White-hall; and in their Private Offices the drama and friction between politics and the machine are theatrically audible. I do not think there is anything quite like it in other countries where, to be sure, they have Directeurs de Cabinet, Chiefs of Staff or political advisers, but where these owe fealty primarily to the Ministers upon whom their tenure of office usually depends. What marks the Private Secretary to a Minister in the British system is his permanence. By that I do not mean that he goes on for ever, but that he does not necessarily come or go with the Minister. With a few exceptions he belongs to the department; he is appointed regardless of his political opinions; he is the hinge between the Minister and his Ministry, and his loyalty is really a double one – to both Minister and department. It is this duality that gives him his exceptional influence; he represents to the Minister the opinion of the Office and to the latter the will of the Minister. Neither commission would carry the same weight if it were not balanced by the other.

'The relations between a Minister and his Secretary', Disraeli wrote in *Endymion,* 'are, or at least should be, among the finest that can subsist between two individuals. Except the married state, there is none in which so great a confidence is involved, in which more forbearance ought to be exercised or more sympathy ought to exist.' (Monty Corry, later Lord Rowton, Disraeli's long-term Private Secretary, was the model for this description.) That was written over a hundred years ago, but I do not think it is very different now, except that with the greater role of government today, and with the larger say of public and parliamentary opinion in foreign affairs, the place where Ministers and officials meet – the Private Office – requires an even more understanding relationship between the two.

Alan Bullock devotes a great deal of attention to the crucial role performed by the Private Office in Bevin's tenure of the Foreign Office.[1] 'Bevin', he writes, 'could only cope with the demands made on him because he was able to rely on a Private Office whose staff were devoted to him.' On the basis of my own experience I would judge this to be a very low-key statement of the contribution made by the Private Office to Bevin and of their devotion to him. Indeed, with travel, the life of a present-day Foreign Secretary becomes increasingly bound up with that of his Private Office which, with its attendant props of files, boxes and machines, moves about the world with him like an itinerant circus.

Amongst the several Private Secretaries it is inevitably the Principal Private Secretary who is the most important. As Lord Strang, a former Permanent Under-Secretary in the FO but never

---

1 Alan Bullock, *Ernest Bevin,* Vol. III (1945–1951), p. 290.

a member of the Private Office, has described it: 'he is the official most frequently in the company of the Secretary of State'.[2] Like Godolphin, 'never in the way, never out of the way',[3] his sheer physical proximity will ensure his influence, provided he is a paragon of tact. He must not excite envy, nor must he appear to usurp the authority of the Permanent Under-Secretary in giving advice whether on policy or appointments. 'The Private Secretary', wrote Tom Jones, whom Lloyd George brought to No. 10 where he pioneered the high, but hidden, role of the modern Private Secretary, 'nurses … a passion for anonymity and secret influence[4]. Restrained in the influence he exerts and prudent in the way he manifests it, he must not become a Svengali, a part that should, I hope, be unlikely to tempt him until we have a Trilby as Foreign Secretary.

I have found much curiosity about what actually happens when one Minister takes over from another. It is an essentially human situation, and there is obviously enough conflict and personal drama inherent in it to stimulate the interest of even the least politically minded person. Confidence between the Minister and his Private Office has to be established. He may want to make changes, whether in staff or procedure. He may need discreet advice about personalities at home and abroad. He may wish to exert himself and manifest his authority forthwith.

---

2 Lord Strang, *The Foreign Office*, p. 160.
3 Charles II's description. Sidney Godolphin, Lord High Treasurer under Queen Anne, made himself indispensable in providing the finances for Marlborough's campaigns.
4 Thomas Jones, *A Diary with Letters*, p. xxi. Tom Jones's actual post was that of Deputy Secretary to the Cabinet.

R. H. S. Crossman has described as follows the speed and unsentimental matter-of-factness in which a change of régime is executed in Whitehall: 'The only operation to which I can compare the Whitehall drill for a change in government is the hospital drill for removing a corpse from the ward and replacing it with a new patient.'[5]

In the autobiography of Hugh Dalton (the first Chancellor of the Exchequer in Attlee's Government), one of the frankest accounts written by a British politician in recent times until Crossman's book smashed all records for indiscretion, advice is given about how a Minister should behave on entering office. He should show his officials that he has a mind of his own: 'Perhaps by refusing some early piece of advice as Arthur Henderson[6] did on his first morning at the FO in 1929, when he was advised to congratulate the Pope and Mussolini on the conclusion of the Lateran Treaty and to refuse Trotsky a visa. Perhaps by making a fuss about the secretarial arrangement?'[7] Yet even without any such instant assertions of authority the take-over by a new Foreign Minister is likely to be a ticklish business, particularly for the Private Secretaries. It was an experience I was to undergo several times.

What generally occurs is something like this. Immediately after his appointment the new Minister telephones the Private Office. He suggests that he comes into the office at such and such a time if that is convenient to the departing Secretary of State.

---

5 R. H. S. Crossman, *The Inside View*, p. 13.
6 Arthur Henderson, Labour politician, Foreign Secretary 1929–31.
7 Hugh Dalton, *High Tide and After*, p. 15.

The latter, unless by chance he is to become Prime Minister or Chancellor of the Exchequer, is not experiencing his finest hour. The *Glanzpunkt* of his career is most distinctly behind him and his heels are hyper-sensitive to the slightest oncoming tread. Besides, after all, documents have to be signed, goodbyes to be said, those photographs of foreign colleagues – the paper currency of statesmen – need to be disposed of, and carefully too, now that they have suddenly assumed an enhanced value as symbols of erstwhile status and respect. The Private Secretaries must be sure to have the requisite number of signed portraits of himself, the departing Minister, including one for the walls of the Private Office. Surely anyone could see that all this must take time. So there is a limit to the speed at which he, the outgoing Minister – for after all he still is technically Minister – can be hustled into the wings.

However, an hour for the new man's entry is eventually agreed upon. There is a Whitehall story from the days of the first Labour Government which shows how necessary are adequate preparations for a new Minister's arrival, particularly after a change of régime. J. H. Thomas[8] apparently turned up at the Colonial Office quite unheralded. There was no one at the door to meet him. A messenger stopped him. He explained that he was the new Secretary of State for the Colonies, upon which the messenger shook his head and said to the colleague beside him: 'Another case of wartime shell-shock, I'm afraid.'

Meanwhile in the Private Office, as soon as the new Minister's

---

8 James Henry Thomas, Labour MP 1910–36, Colonial Secretary in the first Labour Government (1924).

appointment is known, it is off with the old liege, on with the new. There is a note of expectation in the air, and the room wears more than its usual aura of importance. At no other moment can the contrast between the permanence of the official's life and the precariousness of the politician's be more complacently apparent. There is much thumbing of *Who's Who*. The Whitehall grape-vine is hectically tapped for tips, from any other department where he may have worked, on the likes and dislikes and the idiosyncrasies of the new Minister, and, no less important, of those of his wife. The FO is apt to think that the Minister's wife is more important in their life than in that of other departments: apart from giving tea to ambassadresses, she frequently accompanies the Foreign Secretary on his journeys abroad, so she is part of the team. There is a Treasury story that when Mr R. A. Butler was appointed Chancellor of the Exchequer, his wife, the forceful daughter of Samuel Courtauld, telephoned the Private Office immediately. 'If you have any trouble with Rab,' she said, 'don't argue with him, just let me know.'

At the appointed hour the Principal Private Secretary goes to meet the new Secretary of State at the door. Alas, they do not always make for the same door – there are many entrances – and there is often much hurried searching followed by breathless apologies. The new Minister is escorted solemnly into the building, to his own private lift if he has been lucky enough to arrive at the Park Door; if not he would quite likely, in former times, have been taken to the lift in the centre of the building, one of the earliest but finest examples of the stop-go system in Whitehall. It has now been removed like a tooth, leaving a gaping hole in the staircase. But it served admirably to introduce many a visitor to the vagaries of the Foreign Office, to that capricious alternation between dignity and squalor which is the hallmark of the building, as indeed of most public offices and much public life in our country.

Adopting the cheerful tones of a house-agent, the Private Secretary proceeds to show the Minister round his palatial room, with its magnificent view over St James's Park and the Horse Guards.

'Here, sir, is your desk with the inkstand which Lord Curzon objected to ...[9] Yes, your desk and chair face the portrait of George III, but you can have them the other way round and turn your back on him if you like; some Ministers do.'[10]

The Minister begins to pace his domain. The Private Secretary continues his patter.

'That is the window from which Sir Edward Grey spoke about the lamps of Europe ...'

'Yes, of course.'

The Minister knows that.

'And here, sir ...'

---

9 On seeing the inkstand for the first time on becoming Foreign Secretary, Lord Curzon is said to have expostulated: 'In Lord Salisbury's time there stood here an inkstand of alabaster; what is this contraption of glass and brass?' – pronounced to rhyme with gas.

10 Mr George Brown went further. On becoming Foreign Secretary he had George III removed altogether. In his place he installed a fine portrait of Palmerston. Bevin enjoyed having George III there, as it provided a peg for jokes with American visitors. David Owen introduced Oliver Cromwell to the Foreign Secretary's room. Peter Carrington had two Zoffany portraits of Persian merchants hung, for adornment or inspiration. These were still there under Geoffrey Howe, who faced over the mantelpiece a painting of General Jung Bahdour Koowar Ranajee, Prime Minister and Commander-in-Chief of Nepal, at the age of thirty-two. See page 178 for the change under Robin Cook.

At this point it is necessary for the Private Secretary to cover a lot of floor space and somehow to take the Foreign Secretary along with him. With a flourish he opens the door at the far end –

'And here, sir, is your loo.'

He opens the door. The Minister peeps round. The Private Secretary, as if to make him feel at home, throws away a line about its having the best view of any loo in London. The Minister grunts non-committally. The Private Secretary is conscious of the beauties of this loo because the members of the Private Office are accustomed to using it when the Foreign Secretary is out. They do this by age-long prescription, a right they have assumed, without, however, clearing it with the Minister who may well only become aware of it when on some occasion he returns to his room unexpectedly and finds his Private Secretary *in situ*.

'And I, as you know,' the Private Secretary concludes, striding back into the room and pointing to the other end, 'I am your Principal Private Secretary. The three Assistant Private Secretaries are in the room through that swing door. I should like to introduce them to you as soon as possible, but before doing so I'm afraid there's something I must do ...'

The Secretary of State looks surprised. The Private Secretary continues, a little breathlessly:

'Yes, you see, constitutionally, when a new Foreign Secretary arrives, all the Private Secretaries have to submit their resignations so that, if he wishes, he can make his own appointments to his Private Office.'

'Oh,' the Foreign Secretary says, again without commitment. The Private Secretary begins to rush his lines: 'But usually they just carry on, at any rate for the time being.'

'Yes, please do, at any rate for the time being,' the Secretary of State says, visibly relieved; though sometimes the Minister may at this stage announce his intention of bringing in someone from outside, a political adviser – a genus that has become much less shy of late in the Whitehall jungle and that shows no drift to extinction.

A certain amount of confidence is established by the next item: a spot of dual instruction on the elaborate system of bells, buzzers and telephones, which connects the Foreign Secretary's room with the Private Office next door. 'You see, Secretary of State, you can have the bell which rings through to us moved somewhere else if you like. Some Foreign Secretaries like to have it where it can't be seen by visitors, but near enough for them to be able to ring if anyone stays too long. Some want bells all over the place, like fire-alarms on a ship. We're always having to have them shunted about.'

Most Ministers are intrigued to hear about their predecessors, particularly the personal foibles of members of their own Party, provided of course that the proprieties are observed. The Private Secretary must know his place. There must be no transgressing the constitutional line which separates master from servant.

The Private Secretary will be well advised to show respect early on with a new Minister for the essential freemasonry of politicians, their solidarity – yes, their solidarity as human beings, representing the people – in the face of the official machine. But he must also show that he himself belongs to the Minister, as well as to the Office. The offer of resignation was intended to do this in a subtle way.

For the subsequent stage of introduction, the Secretary of State is taken next door to the series of rooms, interconnecting, overcrowded and hot, like greenhouses, which are inhabited by the Private Office staff: the furthest where four shorthand typists hammer frenziedly; the middle one containing half a dozen clerks who have to be able to turn up any telegram, minute or dispatch at a moment's notice; and the nearest, the Private Office, usually occupied by four Private Secretaries. This last is the place where politics and diplomacy come together, Minister and machine interlock, home and abroad meet; a clearing-house for papers, a crossroads, a meeting-point, a bedlam. It is the most exciting room in the whole Foreign Office. There is always something going on there and enough static in the air to produce shock at any time.

A room which is always open to visitors and accustomed to awkward situations, the Private Office has acquired mementoes, pictures, statuary and incongruous gifts from all corners of the globe, that have piled up over the years like deposits in an archaeological site. The eye of the new Foreign Secretary is immediately caught by the engravings and photographs of all his predecessors hung chronologically round the walls. However brief his tenure of office or exiguous his place in history books, he will be immortalized here at least; though, as he looks round, he will not escape noticing how cramped the plots of wall space allowed to recent Ministers are compared with the generous hatchments occupied by Charles James Fox[11] and the early Fathers. Few new visitors to the Private Office fail to observe this remarkable gallery. Many are

11 He was the first Secretary of State (bringing with him Sheridan as Under-Secretary, who was much like a modern Principal Private Secretary). The Foreign Office only came into existence in 1782. Previously foreign business had been conducted by two Secretaries, one for the Northern Department (originally for the Protestant powers); the other for the Southern Department (which covered the Catholic powers and home affairs).

induced to make some passing comment to the Private Secretaries who might well otherwise come to regard the portraits with the detachment due to office furniture. On one occasion, for instance, a doctor called to see the Secretary of State. After looking at the photograph of Arthur Henderson on the wall he said, 'You could see it was not a good life.' As he was wafted into the Minister's room, he left the members of the Private Office wondering uncomfortably how much of a span he had allotted them.

The new Secretary of State will pay a call on each of the four desks occupied by the Private Secretaries – desks laden with telephones and boxes, the hardware of officialdom. After long experience of calling on his constituents, he will find this occasion less embarrassing than do the occupants. Or, he may try to engage everyone in conversation at once, sitting perhaps on the mahogany table in the middle of the room, with his legs dangling to the floor, a posture which may evoke in his audience memories of school, of occasional but gracious visits to the classroom by the headmaster. The Minister will cast an eye around the room: at the red-bound Foreign Office lists; at the high reading-desk covered with the day's newspapers; at the miniature wooden chest which holds the labels of all the departments of the Office, but which looks as if it had really been built for birds' eggs; and all the time he will be conscious of the ceaseless ebb and flow of boxes – some red, some black, some blue and some even yellow; rectangular boxes, flat boxes, long boxes and short boxes, the smallest, very squat and black, and bearing the portentous words Prime Minister, without which it might be taken for a child's plaything or the coffin of some diminutive pet – all of them borne into and out of the Private Office by a conveyor belt of office-keepers.

The small body of specially chosen office-keepers attached to the Private Office and the Secretary of State's room help to give the place a certain dignity which might otherwise escape the notice of visitors. Many an ambassador has been surprised, for instance, by the extraordinary licence allowed to the pigeons around the Foreign Office, whose portals they render so perilous, but they come to accept this in time, perhaps, as a reflection of the English attitude to animals – and foreigners – or at any rate as a manifestation of the well-known British sense of humour, the scourge of the Diplomatic Corps. Once inside the building, the caller will have to pick his way over the tessellated floor, often fragmented like an incomplete jigsaw, past milk bottles and tea trolleys, past peremptory notices announcing, 'Window Cleaning Today' – some sort of code, he naturally presumes – until he arrives at the mural decorations at the top of the Grand Staircase. The paintings either side of the vast doors of the Private Office depict *Britannia Sponsa* conceived as a wild, fair-haired shepherd girl, and *Britannia Nutrix* as the Bride become the Mother.[12] The well-favoured proportions of *Britannia Nutrix* at her most maternal have been known to engage and even excite the attentions of the most blasé diplomat as he hangs his coat on the rickety metal support that those responsible for the running of the building have seen fit to place incongruously in front of this particular mural.

---

12 There are three other paintings alongside showing Britannia in various grandiose guises. All are the work of Sigismund Goetze, a brother-in-law of Alfred Mond, First Commissioner of Works at the time when the Cabinet decided to hang the pictures in the Foreign Office, a decision strongly but vainly opposed by Lord Curzon, a man of discrimination.

But to return to the new Secretary of State's arrival in office: having completed his visit to the Private Office, he will be escorted to the adjoining rooms occupied by the ladies, as the personal assistants, clerks and attendant shorthand typists used to be called in the FO. This may be the most ticklish moment of the whole initiatory process. More personal and less protean in their loyalties than the Private Secretaries, the ladies are inclined to pin up on their walls photographs, cuttings and cartoons of their favourite Minister, and they are reluctant to dismantle these merely because a little matter like a general election has taken place and produced a change of government. In the rapid turnover of Foreign Secretaries which occurred in the years immediately after 1963, many a new Minister found, on visiting this room for the first time, that he had to run the gauntlet of Sir Alec Douglas-Home's features, so enduring was his and Lady Home's hold upon their Private Office staff.

Having met his own immediate entourage, the Secretary of State returns to his room. He may have one or two personal problems he wants to discuss. An anxiety of some Ministers on becoming Foreign Secretary for the first time is whether a knowledge of foreign languages is essential. I always tried to be reassuring on this point. I would say that I thought it mattered little. Most of the Minister's foreign colleagues would probably speak English. For any negotiation there would invariably be an interpreter. Even Gromyko, who spoke English very well, nearly always insisted upon an interpreter for conferences. An imperfect command could, if relied upon, be dangerous.

I do not recall any occasion when the national interest suffered because of the linguistic shortcomings of the Foreign

Secretary. Gordon Walker spoke German extremely fluently, and liked to do so. But Schroeder, his opposite number, also happened to speak English. After one meeting between the two of them there was some hitch in carrying out what was thought to have been agreed, I do not remember exactly what, but one newspaper published a hostile piece saying that it had all been due to Gordon Walker's insistence on speaking German. To many English people there is no conceit worse than that of boasting about foreign languages – understandably, because, as Harold Nicolson has pointed out, it may be due so much to the chance of having been brought up abroad or with a foreign governess, and so little to personal application and skill. Eden was a good linguist, but did not, I suspect, regard it as more than a useful social attribute. Though few could deploy more personal appeal than Eden, he did not believe in personal diplomacy, which he regarded as something of a myth; he believed that countries on the whole were guided by what they perceived to be their eternal interests rather than by personal considerations.

If the Foreign Secretary knows languages better than his officials, this can on occasion cause difficulties for the latter. When Rab, who had got a First at Cambridge in Modern Languages, dispensed with the interpreter for his interview with Chancellor Erhard, the Private Secretary, who was present to take the record and happened to be myself, was left stranded. Rab spoke English and the interpreter who was present translated his words into German for the Chancellor, but at the start of the interview Rab waved aside as unnecessary the interpreting into English of Erhard's German, saying that he had obtained a First Class degree in German at Cambridge University. Erhard spoke with a strong

Bavarian accent. I could pick up little of what he said, which was in any case on some abstruse economic theme. At the end of the meeting I buttonholed the interpreter frantically to ask him to tell me what Erhard had said so that I could make some sort of a record. He was most obliging, for which I overflowed with gratitude. Later when I submitted the record to Rab for approval in the usual way, he, knowing how much more flattering flattery is if expressed in public, generously congratulated me, in the course of some meeting, on having 'got' Erhard. 'I didn't understand a word of what he was saying,' he said.

There is a famous story of Disraeli at the Congress of Berlin which shows the fear of officials at any tendency on the part of Ministers to display their knowledge of foreign languages and the flexibility the Private Secretary (on this occasion Monty Corry) must possess in invoking the help of third parties to deal with their chief at awkward moments. The Prime Minister announced his intention of speaking in French, a possibility which created alarm and despondency among his staff, for they knew that, in spite of a couple of winters spent in Paris in middle life, his French was far from perfect. Corry, being a wise Private Secretary, did not feel it incumbent upon him to remonstrate with his chief, so he invoked the aid of the British Ambassador, Lord Odo Russell, who accepted the somewhat delicate mission. Accordingly, the evening before the Congress was to meet, he caught the Prime Minister just before he went to bed, and said that a dreadful rumour was going round to the effect that he, Disraeli, would speak in French. The Ambassador declared this would be a very great disappointment to the delegates. 'They know', he said, 'that they have here in you the greatest living master of English oratory, and they are looking forward to your speech in English as the intellectual treat of their lives.' Disraeli gravely promised to give the matter due consideration, and the result was that he spoke in English both the next morning and on all the subsequent occasions when he addressed the Congress. Lord Odo afterwards declared that he never knew whether the Prime Minister took the hint or accepted the compliment.[13]

Language, or at any rate the English language as spoken by our political masters, can, however, cause misunderstanding. Persuaded that a foreign colleague can speak English, British Ministers are tempted to talk very fast, often in sporting jargon and sometimes in colloquialisms that are incomprehensible to an outsider. Cricketing metaphors are particularly popular and I have seen many a foreign Minister baffled by being told that he has 'bowled a fast one' or that what he has just said has created 'a sticky wicket'.

No less treacherous is the resort to parables that Ministers may use in international telephone calls in order, they hope, to avoid revealing secrets to someone who may be bugging the line. Thus the Foreign Minister will ring up another and, rather than say outright what weapon it is that he wishes to talk about, will refer to 'the thing we all have in common' or 'you know what I mean, the thing that points upwards'. I know so well the mystification at the other end of the line, the leap to false conclusions or the ready and often fallacious assumption that it is all part of the undying British sense of humour. But I also know that if there are any people left in any doubt about what it is the Minister is talk-

13 Sir Charles Petrie, *The Powers Behind the Prime Minister*, p. 22.

ing about, these are eavesdroppers who will have listened to the explanation the Minister in the end will have had to give about the meaning of his parable.

Having done his best to set at rest any doubts on the scope of languages, and having explained about the official car, the detectives and various other personal questions, of which the most important is, of course, the official flat at No. 1 Carlton Gardens, the Private Secretary will suggest the summoning of the Permanent Under-Secretary: and it will not be long before there is a meeting at which he is introduced to all the senior members of his staff, and then makes a short speech about how he sees foreign policy and what he wants out of the Office. It is customary to refer graciously to the competence of the FO. Long before the Falklands crisis it was the habit of newly arrived Foreign Secretaries to raise a doubt, a very polite and tentative one at this early stage, of course, about the organization of the Office for looking ahead and for dealing with long-term developments. 'I want the Foreign Office to look ahead,' he will say, 'well ahead, and to have plans for the future. We must not be caught napping and have to react hurriedly to crises after they have arisen. We must foresee them.'

As the Secretary of State says these wise words, there will be many equally wise nods from the assembled officials. But there will also no doubt be a number of private glances, exchanged frantically, like distress signals at sea, between the Heads of Departments and Assistant Under-Secretaries. The task of trying to look ahead, so eloquently, yes, and so pressingly stated by the Secretary of State, is after all what they have been attempting to do, and been paid to do, ever since joining the Service many years before. The difficulty has been in getting Ministers to take the necessary decisions which may in the short run prove unpopular politically. The Permanent Under-Secretary may feel moved to say something to the new Minister in answer to his opening remarks. 'Yes, Secretary of State. I know that we are all most grateful to have this outline of your general views on foreign policy. I was also most interested in what you said about the need for looking ahead, and for having adequate machinery in the office for doing so. As a matter of fact we *do* have a Planning staff whose purpose is to do just that …'

'Right,' the Secretary of State will interject. 'Well, let's use it. I don't want to be caught unprepared, as has sometimes happened in the past.'

There will be a slight recurrence of signalling. But for one or two of the officials – those concerned with planning – the Secretary of State's words will bring joy:

Like Snow upon the Desert's dusty face,
Lighting a little hour or two.

The Planning Section have needed just this fillip and for the next few months they will have all the scope they want in attending meetings and in securing the co-operation of the rest of the Office in the completion of their long-misprized Sibylline books. Rab followed it up with a meeting with the Planning staff. He gave them some of his inestimable advice derived from a lifetime in the public service, and from his experience as founder of the Research Centre at the Conservative Central Office. The great thing in research, he told the FO Planners, was to consult as many people as possible. It provided short cuts and saved any amount of time and work.

But the Planners' hopes will probably soon turn to ashes. Before long the Secretary of State will find himself increasingly involved in immediate problems. He has less time to read those far-sighted, those penetrating, but also those inevitably lengthy papers about the future. Anyway it is difficult, he begins to feel, to decide policy now when the circumstances are hypothetical. Foreign policy must surely be pragmatic. That's the way it always has been in Britain; it's the British system, after all. Not too much theory and plenty of hard fact. Besides, any commitment to a specific direction of policy in the future will require discussion with other Ministers. Foreign Secretaries usually come to dread generalized discussions on foreign policy in the Cabinet, where everyone is apt to consider that he knows the subject. Baldwin[14] warned Eden how he must remember that out of his twenty Cabinet colleagues, 'there was probably not more than one who thought he should be Minister of Labour and nineteen who thought they should be Foreign Secretary'.[15] Indeed, difficult though the post is, and rare the politician who has succeeded in it, there can have been few people in public life who would have refused it. But let us examine more closely what is involved, seen at any rate from the angle of the Private Office.

---

14 Stanley Baldwin (1867–1947), British Prime Minister in 1923, 1924–9 and 1935–7.
15 Anthony Eden, *Facing the Dictators*, p. 319.

2

FROM EDEN TO BEVIN; THE POTSDAM CONFERENCE

I was first appointed to Anthony Eden's Private Office in the autumn of 1944, having served a year as Private Secretary to Lord Moyne, Deputy Minister of State in the Middle East. Illness had rendered me unfit for military service and, after a year in the Middle East, I had a relapse which incapacitated me for another twelve months before I was able to join Eden.

At the time, as one of the Assistant Private Secretaries, I was an extremely junior official; yet staying with Eden at his house, Binderton, near Chichester, I was always treated by him with sublime courtesy. Given to gusts of impatience and prone to constitutional irritability, he was nevertheless a most considerate man to those dependent on him – indeed his occasional outbursts had the effect of rendering his politeness more human. Such was his personality that he could get the most out of people – and that applied, incidentally, not just to FO officials, but to foreign statesmen as well. He often said he really felt happiest with soldiers. Glad though he was to return in 1940 to the FO, which, he told me, had the finest staff of officials of any department,[1] he never regretted anything so much as having to give up the War Office at that moment. He loved soldiers; he was interested in military matters; he liked the fact that the job was personal, whereas at the FO there was too much of seeing foreign ambassadors, most of whom were mere automata. And of course nobody realized the difficulty of being Foreign Secretary with Winston butting in all the time from No. 10 – a sense of frustration he was still to find himself suffering from a decade later, when once again he was Foreign Minister and Churchill was Prime Minister.

As a host Eden was impeccable. He wanted to be sure that one had slept well and that the hot-water bottle had been hot, and not leaked. He had to satisfy himself that the bedroom and the library downstairs were warm enough. He was anxious that one should feel at home. It was as though he was deliberately trying to counter any feeling one might have that one was not really a proper guest, but a mere official on duty. At mealtimes there was no maid to serve or clear away. He insisted on doing it himself; he would scarcely let one help.

He hoped one liked his favourite dish, boiled onions. The food was always very good at Binderton, but particularly so after Eden had had a meeting with the Russians. One weekend when Jim Thomas, a close friend of Eden's and for long his Parliamentary Private Secretary, was staying there, we began with caviare and vodka, a gift from Stalin. Jim Thomas said that it was a difficult matter to decide whether the food was best at Binderton, Ditchley

---

1 He was speaking in 1944. Rab, who had a much wider experience of Whitehall than Eden, said exactly the same thing to me twenty years later.

Anthony Eden with war-time gas mask (inscription to the author).

(then owned by Ronald Tree) or at the Cranbornes',[2] a form of competitiveness that appealed to me, despite my tendency to earnestness at the time.

Once when I had travelled down to Binderton alone with Eden late on a Friday evening after a party at the Soviet Embassy, he had much talk on arrival with Maggie, the deaf cook from Yorkshire, who had been with the family for years. Very lucky, he said, to have any cook in wartime; even luckier for the Foreign Secretary to have a deaf one.

'Well, Maggie,' Eden shouted as she brought in the dinner, 'what are you going to give Monsieur Bidault? He's coming to dinner tomorrow night, you know, and he's going to stay the night.'

Maggie did not look over-impressed. She said everything would be prepared all right as usual.

'He's the French Foreign Secretary,' Eden emphasized loudly. 'You're blasé, aren't you, Maggie?' To me in a stage whisper he said laughing, 'If it was Uncle Joe himself she would not turn a hair.'

He explained that as Beatrice and he had not been there, she had done no cooking for four weeks – it must have made her mad.

After dinner Eden talked of his family, his ancestors in Maryland and at Windleston. He brought out albums and family trees and old letters. He gave me his brother's life of his eccentric father to read. He went on to speak of another matter of the heart, Persian poetry. He read out and translated many of his favourite

---

2 Viscount Cranborne (later Marquess of Salisbury), politician, and at this time Secretary of State for Dominion Affairs.

lines. I listened. I admired his skill. I enjoyed the sound of Persian. But being young and, as I have said, earnest, I could not suppress the feeling that perhaps we ought to have been working. In my mind's eye I kept seeing the boxes of work which lay unopened out of sight. But there they remained, while the Persian quatrains continued until we eventually went up to bed around midnight.

We woke up to a beautiful spring morning. The Secretary of State stayed in bed till 1 o'clock pecking at the boxes and reading Ronsard. He was a great reader of the Classics, French, English and, of course, Persian. He was an admirer of the classical in most things, and the owner of some beautiful eighteenth-century furniture, and of paintings and drawings by Augustus John, Duncan Grant, Dunlop and Constable. In the early twenties, before he went into politics, he wrote a paper on the French Impressionists. Nicholas Lawford[3] has described him as an aesthete, which means that he could bring to politics the quality of an artist; something that Harold Macmillan regards as essential to the profession.[4]

I browsed about in the library: apart from the classics, my eye was caught by the very full shelf of Somerset Maugham, and the predictable number of books by journalists on politicians, many of them given by their author, and flatteringly inscribed. Books which the Foreign Secretary received as presents in this way and did not wish to keep, he used to give to the Foreign Office library, or if they were unworthy even of that, they would be sold at Foyle's. The previous day a book had arrived from A. L. Rowse, sent with a most fulsome letter. It lay on Eden's desk awaiting judgement.

---

3 Assistant Private Secretary at the Foreign Office successively to Halifax, Eden and Bevin.
4 TV interview, October 1983.

After Eden was dressed – tweed trousers, suede shoes, a check shirt and silk scarf, the colours in tone and appropriate to a spring morning in Sussex – he scampered into the garden and called to me to stop frowsting in the library and to come out and join him. He was in the highest spirits as he showed me round. 'An old gardener at Gibraltar gave me these plants … I want to build a gazebo here … I'm terrified of my gardener …' He pattered on about anything, alighting now on some point of work, now on the garden. We talked about history and Salisbury's *Essays*: 'By the time I've read all these books I'll be quite a good Foreign Secretary … That field was never ploughed until two years ago … Yes, Bevin could handle Foreign Affairs. No, I don't think a training abroad or deep knowledge of history are really essential. You see, Arthur Henderson is always reputed to have been an excellent Secretary of State, and that was largely because he almost invariably relied on and followed the advice of his officials. I don't believe he ever wrote a word of his own in the FO … It's much safer that way … I can't think why those moles are coming up again …'

Eden was not well during the summer of 1945, and I spent some time with him at Binderton, where he often worked in between visits to his constituency for the electoral campaign. Then in July we all set off for the Potsdam Conference. How stark was the contrast between our comfortable orderly lives in the lake-side villas in the suburb of Babelsberg, not far from the conference, and the havoc of Berlin that lay in ruins nearby. We visited Hitler's bunker and it was uncanny to witness the débris of his and Eva Braun's shelter-rooms there – the dishevelled clothes, the upturned furniture, the scattered photographs and the piles of discarded Iron Crosses – compared with the sedateness of the library and the living-room of our house on the lake. However, our lives were also to be disjointed, though in a very different way.

On Wednesday, 25 July, Churchill and Eden, the leading members of the Caretaker Government that had been in office since the end of the wartime coalition in May, left Potsdam to return to the UK for the declaration of the result of the general election. This had been held up while the votes of Service people were being counted. It was in this pregnant state of the country, between polling day and the count, that our delegation had been operating at the Potsdam Conference. Now, smiling and self-assured, the Prime Minister and Foreign Secretary waved goodbye to the marines, guards, ATS and all the others who had attended on them during the first ten days of the conference, and drove off through the pine trees to the aerodrome.

For months His Britannic Majesty's Government had been urging the governments of Europe to hold as soon as possible 'free and unfettered elections', so that the will of the people could be fairly expressed. The war in Europe was just over and as Eden kept saying we stood 'for rule by the ballot-box, and not by the bullet'. Now, the Prime Minister and he were travelling to England to await the verdict of the electorate so that they could return to Potsdam and pursue their labours in the conference, confirmed and refreshed by the voice of the people.

The flight back was cheerful. After a sleep Eden gossiped to his Private Secretaries about the conference and the election. It is on journeys, particularly by air, that the Private Office really get to know their master. The rest of the Office may well want urgent papers read and decisions taken, but the Private Secretaries will know whether it may not be better to let him have a moment of relaxation, a moment which, incidentally, can be of high value to them. Eden loved talking unguardedly to his entourage. On that flight he was in high spirits and at his most charming. He told the story, which he has recorded in his autobiography, of how Molotov and other Soviet leaders, on saying goodbye at the close of the last meeting, had said how much 'they all hoped for my success'[5] (Byrnes[6] had spoken similarly); it made him feel that he must be a very bad Foreign Secretary. As regards the election, it was a question of majorities: would the Government get a majority of fifty or more; or perhaps less? Would he get a majority in his constituency of over 25,000? If he did, he would give Bob Dixon[7] and me a bottle of champagne. In any case we would all be flying back to Potsdam in less than forty-eight hours.

The results of the election started coming through by 10 o'clock on Thursday morning, 26 July. Eden was in his constituency. All of us in the Private Office were eagerly hanging on to the news. Never modish, the room still had no radio, but people kept dashing in saying, 'Bracken's out, Labour gains 30', then 40 and so on. 'Macmillan's out.' By 11.30 it was clear what the

---

5 Anthony Eden, *Memoirs: The Reckoning*, p. 548.

6 James Byrnes, US Secretary of State 1945–7.

7 Pierson Dixon, Principal Private Secretary to Eden and Bevin, regarded by all who knew him as the paragon of Private Secretaries – intelligent, industrious, self-effacing and human. Later Ambassador to Prague, and to Paris. UK Representative to the UN. He died tragically soon, a week or two after retiring. His son published extracts from his diary: Piers Dixon, *Double Diploma*, 1968.

overall result would be. I rang up Jock Colville,[8] one of the Private Secretaries at No. 10, with whom I had a ten-shilling bet in favour of Labour. 'Don't crow,' he said, as soon as he heard my voice. 'I'll give you your ten shillings now; it's quite clear which way it's going.' We agreed to lunch together.

Just before 1 o'clock I went round to collect him from the annexe of No. 10. 'Come, look at the map-room,' he said. For five years the map-room had formed the backcloth to Churchill's command of the British war effort, by land, sea and air. There, night and day, members of the three Services had stuck coloured pins and flags into the battlefronts of the world. For the election the room had been transformed: instead of war maps and orders of battle there were charts of constituencies and the latest state of the poll. The change in the bearing of the Prime Minister himself was no less striking. Here was a war he had lost; no oratory or inspiration could make any difference now. He was glum. Round the room sat Mrs Churchill, Mary Churchill[9] and Beaverbrook[10] their lengthening faces cupped in their hands. Mary Churchill said, as she saw us, 'The news is very bad.' Churchill said, 'It's very hot in here. Why isn't there more air? Open the windows and let's have some more air.' Inexorably a WAAF officer continued to pin up Labour gains. Jock and I withdrew to our lunch, the Churchills to theirs.

He records at this point how she tried to comfort him by

---

8 J. R. Colville, diplomat, Private Secretary to Neville Chamberlain 1939–40; to Winston Churchill 1940–41, 1943–5 and 1951–8.
9 Mary Churchill, the youngest daughter; married Christopher Soames.
10 Lord Beaverbrook, British newspaper tycoon and member of the War Cabinet 1940–42; a close friend of Churchill.

saying: 'It may well be a blessing in disguise'; to which Churchill replied, 'At the moment it seems quite effectively disguised.'[11]

The end of term had set in throughout Whitehall. No more work was done that day. Energies were turned to speculation. We knew that there were two possibles as Foreign Secretary, Bevin and Dalton.

The next day, Friday, was filled with the same uncertainties, but added to them was the process of winding up Eden's affairs. Before coming down to the Office he rang through from the flat to make sure that there was no new occupant at his desk. He was in jubilant form all day. Apart from his natural buoyancy, he felt no personal affront such as Churchill had suffered. As we cleared out the old letters from his desk, we discussed the cataclysm. Eden thought that the Tories would be out for ten years; there had been a decided left-wing trend for which no amount of election mis-handling was responsible. From his own purely selfish point of view, the result was no bad thing. In his memoirs he admits that before the results had become known he could not suppress 'an unworthy hope that we might lose'.[12] When next the tide of Tory-ism came in, Churchill would no longer be the Party's leader. I asked him whether he would take an active part in opposition from the start and he replied, 'No; we must give them a chance.' He would welcome the rest for a short time, but he knew that he would begin to miss the Office badly before long.

So we cleared up the papers, removed the hats, axed the files and liquidated the correspondence. I asked him to autograph a

---

11 Winston S. Churchill, *The Second World War*, Vol. VI, p. 583.
12 Eden, *Memoirs: The Reckoning*, p. 545.

photograph for me which he did with a generous inscription. I took the bus from Whitehall at about 9 p.m. As we passed Downing Street the conductor said, 'Well, that's the end of old Winnie. At last the British people have woken up.'

Bevin was appointed that night and received the seals of office at the Palace on Saturday morning. He told us afterwards that he had asked Attlee for the Treasury but had told him that he was prepared to serve where he was most wanted. It was only at 6 p.m. on Friday that he had heard that he was to become Foreign Secretary. At the Palace on Saturday he met Dalton. 'I wanted your job,' he said to Dalton. 'And I wanted yours,' replied Dalton.

Bob Dixon and I met Bevin at Northolt airport on Saturday at lunchtime. Two C 54s were waiting, one for the Prime Minister, the other for the Foreign Secretary. For the send-off to Potsdam there was a small party of wives, a large party of cameramen and an even greater throng of cheering RAF ground crew. We climbed into our plane. It was the first flight Bevin had ever made. He sank into his seat puffing. Bob said, 'You have had a pretty busy morning, I'm afraid.' Bevin said, 'Yes, you see I've had all my Transport House stuff to clear up'- then with a broad grin, 'We never expected this to happen.'

'Fasten safety belts, please,' shouted the steward. Bevin struggled and went on struggling, but the two ends of the belt would not meet.

There was a plenary meeting of the three Powers that night at 10 p.m. Talking afterwards to Bob and me, Bevin said that Stalin struck him as 'a man with too much on his mind and that makes him weak'. He also gave us his views on negotiating with foreigners: 'You see, I've had a good deal of experience with foreigners:

before the last war I had to do a good deal of negotiation with ships' captains of all nationalities. These people, Stalin and Truman, are just the same as all Russians and Americans; and dealing with them over foreign affairs is just the same as trying to come to a settlement about unloading a ship. Oh yes, I can handle them.'

We arrived back at the villa to a supper of whiskies and sandwiches. Earlier we had asked Bevin whether he had any views about the food, and whom he would like invited. He clearly was not selective about either – in contrast to Eden.

'I don't care tuppence who you invite to dinner,' he said, 'and I like sandwiches.'

So we had sandwiches for dinner, and various members of the delegation as guests. 'This is a good establishment,' Bevin said, contentedly tucking into the sandwiches. To Alec Cadogan[13] he said, 'Ever been to the Communist Club in Maiden Lane?'

'No,' Cadogan replied, as if suddenly charged with murder.

'Ever met Ben Luzzi?'

'No,' he said with equal emphasis.

'He used to be a Trade Union leader in Vienna before the last war. Ever met Pat Lazarus? Used to see a lot of him in Vienna too.'

This went on for some time, but it did not look as though by the end of the evening Bevin and Cadogan would find that they had many old international acquaintances in common. Bevin did not seem surprised or annoyed. He just went on munching and talking happily.

So ended Bevin's first day as Foreign Secretary, which began

---

13 Sir Alexander Cadogan, Permanent Under-Secretary of State, FO, 1938–46, formerly Ambassador to China, and afterwards permanent UK Representative at the UN.

with a visit to Buckingham Palace and ended with a meeting with Stalin and Molotov. Rarely can anyone have been flung so violently into mid-stream; but Bevin displayed immediately one of his outstanding qualities, confidence in himself and in those who worked most closely with him. He immediately took over the leading role in the British delegation without exciting any resentment from the Prime Minister. Cadogan in his diary described it in this way: 'at Big 3 meetings he does all the talking while Attlee nods his head convulsively and smokes his pipe'.[14]

---

14 *The Diaries of Sir Alexander Cadogan*, p. 778.

3

ERNEST BEVIN

The workaday life in Whitehall of the Private Office is demanding enough, but when I look back it is the time spent away from London, whether at weekends or in travel abroad, that is the most intense and unforgettable.

Weekends with Bevin when he was Foreign Secretary would sometimes begin before lunchtime on Friday when he would have sherry, invariably Harvey's Bristol Cream, brought out of the office cupboard. He would offer a glass or more to whoever came in to see him, pouring it out with plenty of follow-through. He would then push his chair back and let his mind expand, to use his own expression – how to deal with the Russians, or the best way of establishing a proper relationship with Egypt and more generally the need for psychological understanding in dealing with people. 'For instance, if I wanted to get the busmen to agree to something, I'd never approach them just after they'd come off duty when they were tired and hungry. You'd only get turned down. I'd just wait till they'd had their dinner and were feeling better. Then nine times out of ten they'd listen. 'We were

Ernest Bevin at his desk in the Foreign Office (inscription to the author)

accustomed within the Private Office to lump all these sagas together under the term 'hippo stories', and, although I can no longer remember the reason, it seems a good enough description.

There was a favourite Bevin theme about the importance to women of having the right colour-scheme at their place of work: 'You see, when I was at the Ministry of Labour in the war, I had to put up a lot of hostels for girls working in factories. I always saw that there were the right colours on the walls and that the curtains were nice and bright and all that kind of thing. It made a difference. They were happier and worked better. It's simple psychology, you know.'

Bevin was a house-builder *manqué*. He was never happier than when recounting the tale of some new office block constructed in the face of strong ridicule and opposition. He had great theories on where kitchens should be situated, on lighting – he had a pioneer passion for strip lighting – on the 'psychology' of wallpapers, and on the planning of a conference room to deaden jarring nerves. Needless to say he could not wait to get his hands on the Foreign Office, to pull it down and to put up a 'decent', modern building in its place.

Bevin was as attentive to the welfare of the office-keepers as to that of the other members of the Foreign Service. For generations those on duty at the Park Door entrance to the Foreign Office, which is the Foreign Secretary's normal place of entry, had shivered throughout the winter in the biting draught sweeping across the Horse Guards. Nobody had done anything about it until Bevin insisted upon the installation of a glass partition behind which the messengers have since sheltered in somewhat less discomfort. They still talk about their rheumatism and complain of the weather, but Bevin's name is engraved on their hearts as firmly as Edward Grey's is on the plinth of the building just outside.

Bevin, I believe, felt a particular affinity with the office-keepers from the very English, not to say Podsnappian, way in which they would usher some foreign visitor into the Secretary of State's room. Flinging open the great door majestically they would proclaim His Excellency's arrival, as if he were some strange circus artiste from abroad, attaching to him the name of some unheard-of country – an example of the casualness that is as much part of British public life as pomp and tradition.

We heard many wartime Cabinet anecdotes and reflections. 'You had to admit Churchill was human, very human.' Naturally we were told of various triumphs over Enemy No. 1, Max Beaverbrook, who 'did nothing to increase the production of planes, tanks or arms during the war'. He was very emphatic about this. He insisted that Beaverbrook's only contribution had been in securing a speed-up in the repair of aero engines in 1940–41. Beaverbrook, aided and abetted by Churchill, would have strangled the development of radar, had it not been for the efforts and obstinacy of Sir Charles Bruce-Gardner and himself.

With yet another glass of sherry, and without any prospect of lunch, I was listening to Bevin talking about his past in which, to my surprise, he had been unable to find any trace of ambition, when he spoke of his entry into the Trade Union movement: 'It was purely by chance that I became a Trade Union official. I never wanted it. I remember standing on that bridge in Bristol one night about eleven o'clock and old Ben Tillett coming up to me in the dark and saying here was a chance for me to organize the men.' Bevin gave a grunt before continuing: 'Then I never wanted this darned job. I hate it. I wanted to be Chancellor ...'

At 12.30 one Friday morning, 15 March 1946, Bevin signed a financial agreement with representatives of the Swiss Government. It was Bevin's custom, after signing such agreements, to celebrate the occasion by drinking sherry. I got two bottles out of the Government Hospitality Fund, and the office-keeper, Pearce, a man who was to play an important part in the Bevins' life, particularly Mrs Bevin's, handed glasses round assiduously.

After the Swiss had departed, Bevin thought that we might as well finish off the sherry: 'Come on, Henderson,' he said as I started to put some draft telegrams before him for approval. 'There's no need to go easy with government sherry. Have another glass, and give me one too.' Chortling away as I poured it out, he added: 'It's not every day we get £10 million out of the Swiss, is it?'

As we drank I remembered that there was an important Manpower Committee meeting at five in the afternoon. The same sobering thought seemed to strike Bevin, for he put a heavy finger on his diary and drew it down the page. However, he said nothing about the engagement and referred gleefully instead to the visit he was due to pay the following day to Port Talbot. He was to receive the Freedom of the Borough and to kick off in a rugby match.

'Who's coming with me to Port Talbot?' he asked.

'The two detectives,' I replied.

'You'd better come, Henderson. You'd like it. Do you good.'

I said that I would like to very much.

'Yes,' Bevin said with a big grin, 'and it's about time you saw something of the proletariat. You come down wiv me. We'll have the hell of a time wiv all those people and the football match.'

Bevin's capacity for enjoying himself was infectious; I began to feel exhilarated at the prospect of our day at Port Talbot.

'We'll have none of those darned boxes,' he said beaming.

Bob Dixon came in and joined in the sherry and stories. It was characteristic of him that he raised no objection to my going; his loyalty to the Secretary of State, though complete, was never exclusive or selfish, and he took every chance of sharing with the other Private Secretaries some of the more enjoyable sides of Private Office life. Bevin had a lunch engagement for which he eventually departed, booming out, as he waddled into his private lift, which only just encased him, 'I'd like to make the whole darned Foreign Office tight.' The messenger slammed the lift gates to and Bevin disappeared downwards in gales of laughter.

A car with one of the detectives picked me up at 8.15 the following morning outside my flat; or rather, not outside, but some twenty-five yards down the street on the same side. As I got into the back the detective confided, 'We didn't stop right outside your house' – slight pause – 'er, for obvious reasons.' It was too obvious for me, but I let it go and we drove on to collect the Secretary of State and the other detective from Bevin's flat. We found Bevin walking up and down the pavement outside his building oblivious of security, but there was no sign of the detective. He eventually turned up at the station where we arrived in time to catch the 8.55 for South Wales.

We had a carriage to ourselves. Leaving the detectives in charge of the boxes – which had followed us despite Bevin's injunction – we went to the restaurant car for breakfast. Bevin, who in the drive to the station had expressed annoyance with Churchill's Fulton speech ('He thinks he is Prime Minister of the world'), soon recovered his spirits. He tucked into a colossal meal, telling me about all the other breakfasts he had eaten on railway trains. We read the morning papers.

'You know, I think this India business is a wonderful thing,' he said out of the blue. 'I don't believe any country but England could have made a gesture like Clem did in his speech in the House and grant freedom to 400 million people with a wave of the hand. Churchill couldn't have done it. He never understood India and wouldn't listen.'

I didn't say anything. By now we were travelling rhythmically through the Elysian water meadows of the Kennet valley. 'You know, Henderson, we're capturing the moral leadership of the world.'

We returned to the carriage and settled down to work at the boxes, which kept Bevin busy for about two hours. By the time we reached the other side of the Severn tunnel, he had finished all the papers and announced that he was going to sleep. But propped up against one end of the carriage like a porpoise basking on a rock, his eye suddenly caught sight of the countryside through which we were passing, and that meant it was all over with the sleeping and on again with the stories. The valleys, villages and factories outside evoked such memories – of early speeches, strikes and difficult situations triumphantly surmounted – that he had to tell the detectives and me all about them. He remembered the Christian and nicknames of all the Joneses, Davieses and Thomases with whom he had been connected in his adventures. Before we reached Port Talbot he sent me along to the restaurant car to get some whisky.

Immediately after our arrival we had lunch with the Mayor of Port Talbot, the Town Clerk, Councillor Richard Evans, who was also to receive the Freedom of the Borough, and their wives. This took place in a private parlour at the Grand Hotel, a room which was generously adorned with china ornaments, brass pots, fire-irons, and highly coloured gravures of sunsets. The tall, dark

chimneys of the steelworks could be seen through the lace curtains of the windows. The wives seemed to be quite at home, but
they said nothing. Nor did Councillor Richard Evans, whose
shining face exuded pride and happiness. Bevin made up for any
lack of talk in others.

'How's everything?' he asked. 'How's business? Has the new
strip mill started yet?'

He listened, as he always did, to the answers.

Preceded by an orderly column of Borough Councillors and
pursued by a rabble of screaming children, Bevin walked through
the streets to the Grand Cinema where the ceremony of bestow-
ing the Freedom was to be held. Either side of him were the
Mayor and the Town Clerk in full regalia; and flanking them
marched policemen bearing standards. There must have been
close on 2,000 people in the cinema. Bevin was placed upon a
minute, none-too-steady platform, blindingly floodlit. The ceremony began with prayer, including a prayer 'For our industry'.
This was followed by Welsh folk songs sung beautifully by a large
choir of men in evening dress and women in black skirts and
white satin blouses. 'Aren't the Welsh girls lovely?' Bevin whispered to me. Then there were speeches, a great many speeches by
all the local dignitaries, until at last Bevin was called. He said he
had been associated with Port Talbot for forty years, since 1906.
We were better off now than then, better fed and clothed. There
had always been a fine spirit among the people of South Wales.
This had been a great support to him as Minister of Labour. On
foreign affairs he spoke little except to emphasize that he would
go on striving and not be deterred 'by passing events' in his search
for lasting peace. After his speech came the presentation of silver

caskets and scrolls to Bevin and his co-Freemen; then more singing to end up.

Everyone thereupon started surging towards the football ground where Aberavon were to play Swansea. We all went on foot. Prominent in Bevin's retinue was the grandly uniformed, hook-nosed figure of the Chief Constable of Glamorgan. I commented to him on the splendour of the day which was truly mild and sunny. 'Yes,' he said, 'it's always fine in South Wales.'

Bevin kicked off to tremendous applause from the large crowd. During half-time he signed autographs. Otherwise he was left alone and sat, a bulky, brooding, silent figure, throughout the game. He told me afterwards that while watching he had assembled his thoughts for the speech he had to make in the evening.

The match over, we made our way back to the Grand Hotel for tea. Once again I found myself next to the Chief Constable.

'Well, that was a fine game,' I said.

'We always have good football in South Wales,' he replied.

The guests at tea were the same as at lunch, but there was a shifting population of old friends of Bevin's who also came to pay their respects – or rather to greet him on equal terms and exchange yarns.

'Hullo, Ernie, how yer keeping,' was a familiar welcome. They talked of the docks, the mines, the tin works. He listened, laughed and reminisced. I thought of a remark his daughter had once made to me: 'He is always himself.' They were all happy. The Foreign Secretary was one of them in their, and in his, eyes.

In his speech that night at the dinner, Bevin showed his remarkable skill at linking the particular with the general, and the local with the world-wide. Somehow Port Talbot was fitted into his dramatic account of the social, economic and political torments of the world. Their problems were his problems. If they produced more they would be doing more to aid Britain's foreign policy than any amount of oratory or diplomacy on his part. The range of his speech was kaleidoscopic: education, local government, production, famine, foreign trade, Russia, Greece, the USA, UNO, Vyshinsky and the speech Churchill had just made at Fulton.

It was convincing and moving and appropriate. He left the dinner to loud applause and was cheered by a big crowd as he got into his car to drive to Cardiff for the night. He was temporarily exhausted, but happy. In the car he said to me: 'You know, it's worth more to me than all the wealth or fame or anything in the world, to feel that all those people really love me. I suppose I'm sentimental at times.' Then he added, shifting his bulk a little: 'It's not like Winston with all that doin' the V sign and standin' up in open cars. This is genuine.'

When we reached the Angel Hotel, Cardiff, the Chief Constable was there to usher us into a private sitting-room. I left them talking over a bottle of whisky and went to my room to go to bed. Just as I was getting into bed, I heard Bevin's familiar tread outside.

'Come on, lad,' he said, putting his head round the door, 'the Constable has gone. Let's have one more drink and a chat before we turn in.'

So I went back to the sitting-room. Bevin's deep well of stories was not yet dry. And so for another half-hour of this very long day we talked about pitch-cancer amongst coal workers, dermatitis amongst flour millers and gastritis amongst bus drivers. At last, at last, even Bevin's stamina was feeling the strain. I went with him to his room. Outside the door he kicked off his still-tied shoes, leaving them in the passage. He waddled bare-foot into his room, saying 'Good night, lad.'

The next morning we had a long car drive to a house near Bourne End owned by Bevin's film-producer friend Del Giudice. Mrs Bevin had gone down there the previous day. She loved it there, he said. He was glad she had not come to Port Talbot with us: it would have been too long a day for her; she would only have caught a cold at the football match and he would have had her in bed for a fortnight.

Somehow during the car drive the conversation turned to a leading London political hostess of the time. 'She's an awfully silly person,' Bevin said. 'I had to sit next to her at a lunch the other day and do you know what darned silly thing she said to me?' I listened surprised because he was so rarely critical of people personally. He went on, mocking the hostess's affected way of talking. 'She said, "Mr Bevin, I'm very annoyed with you because I think you like Sir Stafford Cripps more than my husband." Now,' Bevin went on indignantly, 'did you ever hear such darned nonsense? So I said, "Do you really think we men go about workin' out which of the others we like best?"'

From there he went on to censure the whole world of London society, some of which still centred on the Dorchester Hotel where it had taken refuge from the air raids during the war. His heart sagged when he had to attend a lunch or dinner with them. 'They don't stand for nothing. But', he added a little dolefully, 'the trouble is the Mrs rather likes it.'

He spoke of Jimmy Thomas and Ramsay MacDonald, but

without bitterness. 'When a man goes bad, like Jimmy Thomas or MacDonald, we just write him off. We don't go on talking about him or running him down. That's where the rest of the Labour Party is different from the intellectuals, who never stop criticizing when a man has made an awful mistake.'

All this talk was particularly interesting to me at the time. There had been many suggestions in the Press recently that Bevin, exasperated by the extreme Left, would part company with the Labour Party one day and join forces with the left wing of the Tory Party, either to form a coalition or a new party. Everything he had said and done that weekend confirmed me in my conviction that he would never take a step of that kind. It was not merely that the Labour Party was an integral part of his being, and that he himself could never change; but he believed, as a matter of pride, that Labour, and he himself in particular, could govern the country without the Tories, and even better than the Tories. It would have been quite out of keeping with his monolithic and dependable character for him to have renounced the habits of a lifetime.

After we had been driving for about an hour we turned off the main road and stopped outside a row of council houses. Bevin wanted to call on his brother, who was eighty-seven. After he had been inside a few minutes he reappeared to fetch the silver casket from Port Talbot which he wanted to show his brother. He stayed with him about three-quarters of an hour, and when he eventually emerged he was met by a throng of children asking for his autograph. He signed, if not easily, at any rate willingly. I never knew him to refuse an autograph.

Bevin told me that his brother had been a butcher all his life.

He had never seen much of him, or of his two other brothers who were also older. His mother had died when he was seven and he had never known his father. Brought up by his sister, he had started work at the age of ten and never received any formal education since that time. He had been an errand boy, train driver, farmer and many other things before becoming a Trade Union official in his early twenties. We drove near a village called Tockington where I used to go often as a child to stay with the parents of the girl who looked after us. Bevin knew it well. He had delivered ginger beer there by pony-trap.

As we drove over the Cotswolds Bevin revealed that he had been a keen walker in his youth. It was the only exercise he had taken for pleasure. At the age of twenty-one he had developed some glandular trouble which left him for life with a great roll of fat round his middle. When motoring for the Union he had often stopped the car on a fine morning and walked fast for eight or ten miles.

The doors of Del Giudice's stockbroker Tudor house, which we reached in time for lunch, were opened by two watery-eyed footmen. Del greeted us with soft yet demonstrative handshakes, and a faint smell of perfume. He was wearing loud-check tweeds and thick-rimmed, dark tortoiseshell glasses. He exuded hospitality. He led us over deep-pile carpets and between enormous bowlfuls of mauve tulips to the drawing-room. The house party were already a little tight. They pressed cocktails on us and congratulated Bevin on his Freedom. Mrs Bevin shouted merrily to me through the ether: 'Hello, Henderson, we're having a lovely time.' Del, who had just returned from a visit to the USA, produced a box of a hundred cigars and a trousseau of ties, socks and coloured braces, all of which he gave Bevin.

We drifted alcoholically into lunch. Del was most solicitous about everyone, particularly Bevin. He wanted to be sure he was enjoying every mouthful of food and drink. At one moment he jumped up from his chair and came hurrying round to Bevin's side to ask him if he would like him to clean his spectacles. Bevin removed them and Del slid from the dining-room in search of a special leather.

As the company tired of eating and drinking there was murmur of a film to be shown in Del's barn. We staggered for our overcoats.

'You must stay, Henderson,' Bevin insisted. 'I want you to see Del's barn.'

'Yes, it's a lovely barn,' Mrs Bevin said.

She asked Del to take us in his car, but in the end we walked the hundred yards. The barn was certainly worth the detour. From the outside it did not make much pretence at age, but no Tudor effort was spared within: beams as numerous as zebra stripes, plenty of oak and iron-work, electric logs in the grate, and all round the walls antlers and tiger skins. There was also a bar. The lights of the barn went out and cigars were handed round as the Dolly Sisters came on the screen.

After the film footmen served tea in the bar. Del and the Foreign Secretary talked about their insides and, at the former's request, I agreed to arrange for Bevin to see a certain Madame X in London the following day. 'It's only a lavage,' Del confided to me, 'but it'll cleanse the whole business. Royalty and lots of nice people go there. It's very clean.' Bevin duly went there the next evening; but I failed to ask him how the lavage had gone, and he never mentioned it.

By the time tea was over the house party were ready for another film. But Bevin and I went back to the house to do some
work on the fresh consignment of boxes that had arrived from
London. The day's activities had not provided the ideal prelude to
the task of deciding about the future level of German industry.
However, I got the gist of what Bevin wanted and returned to
London by car. During the journey I reflected on the curious contrast for Bevin between his old pals in South Wales with their
working-class solidarity and this new film-producer acquain-
tance with his neo-Tudor luxury. Del Giudice was not a British
aristocrat trying to corrupt him – an overriding fear among
Labour politicians since the debacle of MacDonald – he was a
self-made man like himself and the fact that he was an Italian
somehow made the relationship easier. It could not be denied
that Bevin liked food and drink, and he said to me once that he
would never have got where he did, had the good things of life
been available to him when he was a young man. But more than
anything, I think he mixed with people like Del to please Mrs
Bevin. He was always most considerate towards her, as well as patient and understanding.

I once spent part of a weekend with Bevin aboard a yacht. It
was in the late summer of 1946. He had been taken ill one evening
in London and had passed a very bad night. His doctor had had
to give him oxygen; everything was wrong with him; heart,
blood-pressure, digestion. There was nothing for it but to get him
away, so Dr McCall had taken him down to Fareham and installed
him on his small yacht.

Bevin stole ashore one morning and rang us up in the office to
find out how things were going. Attlee had taken his place as

leader of the UK delegation to the Peace Conference in Paris. What was he doing? The Cabinet had been struggling with a series of international problems: Palestine, Persia, India and, closest to Bevin's heart, Egypt. How was the Cabinet making out? We told him that Ministers had been considering the instructions to be sent to Lord Stansgate, then in charge of the British team in Alexandria negotiating a revision of the Anglo-Egyptian Treaty. Bevin wanted to know what the Cabinet had decided. As soon as we informed him, he expressed disagreement. He thought that the Cabinet were giving away too much. He would have to take a hand himself. He must see all the papers. Could someone bring them to him? Meanwhile no telegram was to be dispatched in implementation of the Cabinet's decisions.

I collected all the papers, briefed myself with the Department, and made off for Fareham. Dr McCall collected me at the Red Lion Hotel at 5 p.m. He told me that Bevin had made a remarkable recovery; but it had been a near thing that night in London. 'I just had to get him away,' the doctor said, 'I had to get him away on his own. The yacht seemed the only answer.' We went by dinghy to the yacht which lay half a mile up the Fareham estuary. Bevin was in the cabin when we went aboard. He assured me that all was well with his health, but there was a blue tinge in his face which contrasted with McCall's red glow. However, he was very calm and suggested that we should all have a cup of tea together, before getting the papers out. I told him the news from London. He did not much like the thought of anyone's deputizing for him, not even Attlee; but he listened attentively, seated on one of the bunks, his big hands clutching his enormous knees. Suddenly he broke out: 'You know, I'm not conceited, but I really think the darned Cabinet goes to pieces when I'm not there. I can't afford to be away. How lucky that I rang up this morning. I had a funny feeling that something was going wrong. My instinct told me that.'

He soon insisted on looking at the papers, which now became part of the tea-party. It was agreed that I should go ashore and telephone the Office to say that I would be in touch the following evening about Egypt. We would all spend the night on board, sail in the Solent the following day and return to the Hamble, whence I would get a car to take me to London with the papers that night. 'It'll do you good, a bit of a sail,' Bevin said. McCall pressed me in advance to agree to stay a second night as well. I muttered that I would have to get back to send off some telegrams. Bevin said: 'No, he better go back tomorrow. He's sure to be going out with a girl on Saturday night, or something.'

I went ashore and rang up the FO as arranged. We then went through the papers thoroughly. By this time we were ready for the dinner of dried egg and steak which McCall's skipper cooked for us. We drank whisky moderately. Bevin decided that we should do no more work that night. We talked of his health. He said that that night last week had been the first time in his life when he felt he was nearly dying. I said we hoped to arrange a regular after-noon rest in the office. He said he needed another Parliamentary Secretary. We put the wireless on. Bevin wanted to hear a pro-gramme of Caruso, due at 10.30. With a good deal of chaff we climbed into our bunks. We slept as well as the close quarters would permit. Bevin was not a quiet sleeper.

The next morning, as we all had cups of tea around 6.30 a.m., Bevin announced that he had done a good deal of thinking during the night. I said nothing. After breakfast he basked in the sun on deck for a while. This made him reflect on his hard lot. He had no country house, and even when Dorneywood did become available he wouldn't want to go there: 'It's an awful place. Full of very old stuff that Courtauld-Thomson's collected for ages. I couldn't live with that.' He bemoaned his poverty as a Cabinet Minister. He had been better off with the Union. I took the opportunity to tell him what I earned. 'A good deal less than a tin-plate worker in South Wales,' he said indignantly.

By the afternoon we were sailing through Portsmouth Harbour and the Solent to Hamble. It was a beautiful day. Bevin sat happily on deck. People on other yachts passing close-by glanced our way. 'That's a familiar figure,' they seemed to say to themselves, but quickly turned away as if to dismiss the idea. 'No, it can't be, of course not.'

We went below to resume work on Egypt in the cabin. He was worried about the proposed drafting of Article 2 of the Treaty relating to the circumstances in which HMG would be entitled to re-enter Egyptian territory after evacuation of the country. He did not like the suggested formula for the date of evacuation. He stayed scribbling alternative drafts, applying his unique technique of holding the pen between his two fingers, and then just letting his hand shake. I also made an attempt to write down the sense of what he wanted to convey. We then compared drafts. Without difficulty we hit on the wording he was searching for. I incorporated this in draft telegrams and packed the box up ready for return to London.[1]

---

1 Bevin's intervention led eventually to the visit to London in October 1946 of the Egyptian Prime Minister (Sidqi) and Foreign Minister, during which

I should interpolate that the Private Secretaries had come to pride themselves on their technique of ghost-writing for Bevin. In their drafts they tried to preserve his idiosyncratic syntax while leaving no doubt about the meaning. Lawford,[2] who stayed on as Assistant Private Secretary for a short time after Eden left, became a master Bevin draftsman. He would dash off a Bevin telegram with aplomb, and the other Private Secretaries came to model themselves on his style rather than on the true Bevin, rather as a portrait painter will sometimes prefer to work from a photograph than from real life.

Bevin accepted these imitations; and he recognized Lawford's skill, but he was not flattered, and at times showed a touching awareness of his own shortcomings. 'You know,' he would say, 'it's no advantage not being educated. It's an awful handicap. I've often thought that this is the only job I could do, in the Foreign Office.' But these moods of self-criticism would soon pass. 'It's a funny thing,' he sometimes soliloquized, holding his pen between his first two fingers and scratching illegibly, 'but my trouble is that my mind goes so fast that my pen can't keep up.' Bob Dixon would express surprise to me afterwards, a tolerant, amused surprise, that it never seemed to occur to him that his trouble was that he wrote exceedingly slowly. In the same buoyant mood, Bevin would frequently relate his reply to King George VI's question about how he had acquired his great knowledge of the world

---

agreement was reached on a draft Treaty. Unfortunately Sidqi on his return to Egypt was unable to secure sufficient support for ratification and, as a result, he resigned. That was the end of the draft Treaty, as it was also the cause of lasting disappointment to Bevin.

2 See his brilliant memoir, 'Three Ministers', in the *Cornhill*, Winter 1956–7.

– that it had been 'plucked from the hedgerows of experience'.

Bevin took things in much less easily by reading than by word of mouth. This caused him, particularly in his early days at the Foreign Office, to attach great weight to the value of conferences, and he tended to think that people, or their representatives, would be readier to agree the more they heard the other side's point of view. These feelings played some part, I suspected at the time, in his decision in 1946 to call a conference about Palestine to be attended by both Arabs and Jews. When the conference met Bevin appeared to be struck, as if by some new element, by the force of verbal argument on either side, although mountains of submissions had been made to him showing clearly that the Jews would accept nothing less than Partition and that the Arabs would agree to nothing more than the 1939 White Paper.

I have frequently been struck by the habitual dislike of Foreign Secretaries for Chequers. When he was Foreign Secretary, Eden did his best never to spend a night there. Even Bevin, whose relations with Attlee were totally uncomplicated, resented the place. Shortly after his return from the UN General Assembly in New York in December 1946, Bevin motored down to Chequers one Saturday morning for a general talk. I went with him. During the drive we discussed everything: Egypt, Palestine,[3] Stalin, the Foreign Secretary's flat, and the Labour rebels in the House of Commons. It was one of the joys of working for Bevin that he talked about everything with his staff, and his Private Office shared all:

---

3 He said that he had decided that we ought to hand the Mandate back to the UN. On the drive home he told me that the PM had come to the same conclusion independently. He had said 'Churchill is right; we should clear out of Palestine.'

his thoughts, his feelings, his ups and downs and of course his anecdotes, his likes and dislikes. At that moment he did not like the left wing of the Labour Party in the least. They had been gunning for him for months. Their views had found regular expression in the *New Statesman*. Not long before, I had been to see him one weekend at his flat to take a box of papers. I had also taken along a copy of the *New Statesman* containing a particularly critical article about his foreign policy. I gave it to him to read. He read it, chewing on his cheek. 'Written with a fat head,' he said, handing it back without further comment.

While he had been in New York that autumn, a group of Labour MPs, of whom Dick Crossman was the ringleader, had led an attack on his policy in the House of Commons. Hector McNeil, then Parliamentary Secretary in the Foreign Office, had telephoned Bevin from London one evening to tell him about the revolt. I happened to be on duty at the time and listened in to the conversation, which went like this:

BEVIN: 'Who are they?'

MCNEIL: 'There are quite a number of them.'

BEVIN: 'Go on, give me their names.'

MCNEIL: 'Well there's X.'

BEVIN: 'I'll break him.'

MCNEIL: 'And Y.'

BEVIN: 'I'll break him.'

MCNEIL: 'And Z.'

BEVIN: 'I'll break him.'

and so on through the whole list of rebels. There was not one to be left unbroken.

But I am digressing from the journey to Chequers at the end

of 1946. In the car, his mood confident and relaxed, Bevin referred to the next debate in the House. The rebels would not have a leg to stand on. He would crush them. In New York the Russians had realized that he was not going to give way on anything. 'Molotov must have had a shock when he saw I didn't take no notice of the fuss in the House and all that business.' By now Bevin was gurgling triumphantly: 'I think Stalin's decided that he had better come to terms with me.' Bevin was apt to see everything in terms of an actual or potential negotiation.

However, as we drove up to the door of Chequers his spirits obviously sank. 'I don't like this place much,' he said, 'it's Oliver Cromwell and all that kind of thing.' I was reminded of his bad mood after his last visit to Chequers when he had flown home from the Paris Peace Conference for discussions with the PM. He had fulminated afterwards about the whole atmosphere 'with Clem playing croquet and never askin' me once how I was'. To Roddie Barclay who was his Principal Private Secretary at a later stage he complained bitterly about Chequers. 'You don't get enough to eat; they give you sherry in glasses the size of thimbles and the only warm room in the house is the lavatory.'[4]

We were met at the door by John Addis, one of the Private Secretaries from No. 10, who was doing weekend duty at Chequers. A Foreign Office man, seconded to No. 10, he clearly shared the Secretary of State's feelings about the place and he greeted us as though we had brought him deliverance after long siege. He showed the Secretary of State straight into the PM's study and proceeded to let off steam. 'I hate it from top to bottom,' he said.

---

4 Sir Roderick Barclay, *Ernest Bevin and the Foreign Office*, p. 44.

'I hate the false panelling and the phoney windows, the courtyard converted into a drawing-room and the draughts everywhere.' He also explained how uncomfortable he found the social position of the Private Secretary on duty: it was equivalent to that of a governess or tutor: he attended all meals, except tea, did not speak unless spoken to, and kept strictly to his room or the garden, unless asked to take part in some game with the family.

The lunch was very much a family affair. There was no general conversation. Bevin hardly spoke to Mrs Attlee or to one of the daughters who sat on his other side. The Prime Minister was no more communicative than usual. There was suddenly a complete silence over the table. Mrs Attlee burst out laughing, followed by the children who looked at their watches. It was ten minutes to the hour, they all exclaimed, and exactly the same thing had happened the day before. Mrs Attlee became involved in an argument with the Prime Minister about the time they got up that morning and the accuracy of their respective watches. The Prime Minister gave way. Bevin looked glum. He was chewing away on the inside of his cheek.

Lunch over, the PM started showing off the furniture in the dining-room. He pointed to a chest made from a tree planted in the reign of King Stephen. 'When was it planted?' somebody asked. 'In King Stephen's reign, 1135–1154,' he fired back. He told us the age of the carpets and we all admired them. Bevin said: 'The funny thing is they're all made by children.' Several members of the Attlee family looked incredulous. 'Yes, they are,' Bevin insisted. 'I knew a bit about the carpet industry at one time. And all the best carpets are made at Birkenhead. They sell them to Persia who sells them back to us and the Americans at a high price.' Having imparted this surprising piece of information he waddled from the dining-room.

He and Attlee had another work session together and at about 4 p.m. we drove off home without waiting for tea. There was none of the euphoria of the outward journey. Bevin said that his talk with Attlee on so many different problems had tired him. He was chewing hard. He was happy to get back to London.

4

THE CIRCUS ON THE MOVE;
FAREWELL TO BEVIN

Weekends with the Minister may be life-enhancing enough, particularly in retrospect, but the quintessence of FO Private Office
existence is travel abroad for meetings and conferences – circus
life, as I have called it, with everybody and everything on the
move in mobile compartments, and a good deal of trapeze-like
tension. 'I have found a new pleasure in life,' wrote Harold Nicolson, describing a wartime tour as a junior Minister: 'travelling
with a Private Secretary. One just walks about in a fur coat and
things get done.'[1] Alan Bullock has made a more weighty comment saying that the 'work of the Private Office was at its most
hectic in the middle of conferences abroad when all hours had to
be worked and feats of improvisation performed behind the
scenes'.[2]

The first peacetime conference I attended was the Paris Peace

---

1 Harold Nicolson, *Diaries and Letters 1939–45*, p. 132. The Private Secretary
referred to was Alan Hodge, later co-editor with Peter Quennell of *History
Today*.
2 Bullock, *Ernest Bevin*, Vol. III, p. 290.

Conference which opened in May 1946. The British delegation was housed in the Hotel George V. Paris was still short of food, and much of what we ate had to be brought from England – dried eggs, for instance, the taste of which I still have no difficulty in recalling. Members of the party would slip out furtively from time to time to go to a black market restaurant. There was a favourite, but fantastically expensive, bistro in Les Halles where I had soupe d'oignon for the first, and most memorable, time. Our hotel was said to be full of film stars, including Marlene Dietrich, and this generated much excitement, though I myself never set eyes upon any of them. But what I suppose imprinted this visit most indelibly on my memory was the beauty of Paris that first peacetime spring, where, strolling by the Seine or in the Faubourg Saint Germain, you could feel the whole city coming to life again after the Occupation, like a Japanese flower unfolding in water.

The Bevins, the Dixons and I occupied a corridor of rooms on the first floor, where we set up the Private Office and installed all our boxes of papers. Two French detectives were on watch day and night to look after Bevin. We had a rota of guards of our own. Here, on this corridor, work and play, official and private life, foreign affairs and human relations were all mixed up together and pursued inseparably, so effectively in fact that before long John Henniker, Assistant Private Secretary, became engaged to Osla Benning who was in charge of administration, with particular responsibility for making the Secretary of State and his Private Office comfortable.

Bob Dixon and I had breakfast together each morning. The day's plans would be discussed, the telegrams which had come in during the night would be sorted, and the large crop of ideas which Bevin had given forth over dinner the previous evening would be winnowed so that those worth following up could be committed to paper and referred to the appropriate department. Then at about 9 a.m. the telephone would go. It was Duff Cooper wanting to know the time of the morning meeting, which invariably took place at 10 a. m. At these meetings the members of the delegation attending the various committees of the conference gave reports on how things were progressing on their different subjects, and there would be a general discussion on the day's work ahead. It was apt to be desultory. Few were at their best at this hour of the morning, often after a late night when quantities of drink had made up for shortages of food. Seated beside the Secretary of State, Duff Cooper invariably nodded off. One evening over drinks this habit was alluded to by a member of the delegation in Bevin's hearing. 'Yes, I know,' he said, 'but you know I can't help liking Duff. He doesn't care a damn what I think of him.'

Lady Diana cared quite a bit, and was assiduous in sending flowers round to the Bevins' suite in the hotel. 'She's a cunning old thing,' Bob muttered to me one morning when a particularly affecting bouquet had arrived.

After the meeting we all rushed off to the Palais du Luxembourg for the conference. Bevin was driven there in a vast Daimler escorted by French police cars and motor cyclists, the whole cortège moving at great speed and with much noise. Bevin asked us to try to eliminate the motor cyclists. He hated ostentation. The whole idea of interfering with the normal life and movement of a city in order to get to a conference five minutes early was abhorrent to him. But the French security authorities would not agree, so the commotion continued.

Ministers are inclined by nature to be optimistic, and this mood usually governs them at the start of conferences. Bevin was more than life-size in this respect and showed a confidence which certainly seemed justified by the easy manner in which things went at the opening. The US government and ourselves had long been pressing the Soviet government to agree that the French should be allowed to take part in the discussions on all the Peace Treaties, but Moscow objected, and their negative attitude to the French had been the cause of the breakdown of the meeting of Foreign Ministers in London the previous September. In Moscow in December the Americans and ourselves had given way to the Russians on this point, but then suddenly, five months later in Paris, we found that the Russians had changed their position and were prepared to have the French in the meetings on all the treaties. In private talk with Bob and me Bevin leapt to conclusions on the basis of the Soviet shift. 'Things are on the move,' he confided to us gleefully. 'I can tell they want a settlement.' We did not look entirely convinced and he went on, 'Molotov can't go home with a failure.'

However, within a fortnight Molotov was back on his old stone wall. There was virtual deadlock on all important points: Trieste, the Italian colonies, the Dodecanese, Italian reparations, Hungarian reparations, and war criminals in Italy and the Balkans – problems which were not to be solved without a great deal of patient slogging. Nor, apart from Soviet obstruction, was progress helped by the inherent jealousy of politicians, their suspicions of each other's motives, and their conviction that the other fellow was trying to hog the limelight. Bevin would say over the brandy late in the evening, 'I could see as soon as that fellow

Byrnes started talking about a trusteeship for Italy that he was thinking of LaGuardia and the Italians in New York.' I am sure that the other Foreign Secretaries also looked for an *arrière-pensée* in anything that Bevin proposed; and if no specific political motive stood out from some suggestion he made, the suspicion would fall on him, as it did on his colleagues in Bevin's mind, that his purpose was the general one of securing credit for breaking the deadlock.

Imagine the scene: each Foreign Minister has five advisers, sitting either side of him at the conference table, and looking as though butter would not melt in their mouths. Behind this front line are throngs of officials balancing papers on their knees. Every word spoken has to be translated into two other languages. There are many statements read out from previously prepared documents and then translated laboriously. There is the debate and the unrehearsed arguments. Nobody smiles, everyone mumbles. There is much inscrutable glancing at the ceiling. The atmosphere is smoky. There is a set pattern to the play, which would be like a giant poker game were it not all so predictable. It is tedious and unhealthy, though, after the auspicious start, it is perhaps more disappointing than most because of the high hopes in the world outside, that, with the ending of World War II, a new era of international co-operation, a new stage of diplomacy, would surely begin. But it is no better than other such meetings, except perhaps that among most of the participants there are no illusions about this most unchanging of all trades.

While morning drags on at the Palais du Luxembourg, back at the hotel Mrs Bevin is preparing to go out to look at the Paris shops which are gallantly bedecking themselves after the

Occupation. She is accompanied, perhaps by Ismene Dixon (Bob Dixon's wife), more probably by Pearce. Very early on in her reign at the FO Mrs Bevin perceived the importance of the office-keepers. Amongst those attached to the Private Office at this time was this square, bullheaded figure, Pearce, with the presence and voice of a sergeant major. He had made himself so indispensable to the Bevins that he was included in the FO team for the conference. Puffing his way along the corridors of the hotel, frequently laden with parcels and bearing important information about the food situation and the best things to bring over in the diplomatic bag, he was not inhibited from giving clear orders to the French servants in parade-ground English, so that no one in the hotel remained for long in any doubt that the British had arrived and that, incidentally, they had not lost the war. Never out of the way, Pearce proved invaluable to Mrs Bevin in Paris. He took her shopping; he carried her parcels; and he told her how to deal with the French – a relief to the Private Office which therefore did not have to provide an interpreter. Mrs Bevin showed her respect and gratitude by referring to him always as '*Mr* Pearce'. Through the thin door of the Private Office which led into the Bevins' sitting-room, she could frequently be heard saying, 'Mr Pearce, go and ask Henderson to see me', or, 'Mr Pearce, go and tell Dixon that ...'; and the old charger would come short-winded into our room to deliver loudly some important message.

Pearce certainly earned his place in the team when it came to our departure from Paris. Though Mrs Bevin had been packing and re-packing for weeks, she had quite failed to get everything into her suitcases, which were overflowing dreadfully with

'Ernest's things', as she told us. She sent for Bevin, who was busy with some last minute discussions in his office, to ask him to come and sit on the cases, as was his custom, so we were assured. Bevin, who never lacked a proper sense of priorities, waddled off to deal with the crisis. But for some reason he had lost his usual touch and the cases refused to close. So Mr Pearce moved in, and spent a happy and triumphant last half-hour in Paris bouncing on the luggage.

Bevin's health was not good in Paris and, on doctor's orders, we tried to discourage him from having people to meals in the hotel, when there was no official function. But as the time for dinner approached he would nearly always say, 'No, let's have a few people in.' I think he really loved people, which was why he was so genuinely compassionate. 'Poor humanity' was a favourite aside as he dealt with some problem affecting, as he realized, not just frontiers, but people's lives. But he was also sociable, and what he liked best was to sit for hours at the dinner-table after the meal was over, telling stories and drinking brandy. One evening he suddenly said, 'I wonder if the Russians are having a time like this.' Then he looked across the dinner-table at Frank Roberts, at that time Minister in Moscow, who was in Paris for the conference, and asked, 'Do they ever relax – Molotov and those people?' Roberts replied that he thought that the Soviet leaders were the only examples in the world of really whole-time professional politicians. They worked, literally day and night, and allowed themselves no relaxation. Bevin chewed the inside of his cheek.

Compared with the US, French and British delegates, the Soviet officials attending the conference struck a sombre note in Paris that spring. I doubt whether the rest of us did sufficient justice to the appalling deprivations they and their country had gone through during the war. We were apt to look upon their grey, puffy faces, and their grey, square suits, with a certain condescension. They scowled back at us, huddled together in groups at all the parties. The Duff Coopers gave an extravagantly grand dance to mark the conference, with all the glitter and incongruities of which only they could have been capable. The Russians stood in the corners, hunching their broad shoulders, like guests invited graciously but against their will from the country. The Duff Coopers' friends, some of whose activities during the Occupation were a matter of discussion by others, and several of whom had come over from London just for the occasion, occupied the centre of the stage. There was great eagerness amongst the latter to meet the Russians and several asked me to effect an introduction much as if they were asking to be taken to a side-show at a fair. High-coloured, voluble and satanic-looking, Vyshinsky was the centre of interest, and I achieved some sort of social breakthrough by bringing him and Lady Cunard together. They understood each other perfectly.

I spent a long time with Bevin in New York for the first meeting of the UN General Assembly, which took place there in the autumn of 1946. The British delegation were housed in the Waldorf Astoria, very comfortable and very grand, but so expensive that they could not afford even to have breakfast there. In the entry of his diary for Thursday, 14 November 1946, Bob Dixon has given a good description of our lives in New York:

> The pressure is becoming appalling, and Niko and I are finding
> it hard to keep our heads above water. We are getting entangled

on the UNO side (veto, Spain, disarmament, etc.) which is a
heavy burden on top of the Council of Foreign Ministers, with
Trieste at its supreme crisis and all the general FO work,
especially Egypt and Palestine, with which we continue to deal.
This in addition to our normal work of speech-writing,
appointments and the barrage of public relations problems. We
are saved by our meals out, wonderful food, and the excitement
of a walk along 5th Avenue.[3]

Bevin was highly unpopular in New York at the time because
of his attitude to the Jewish case in Palestine. This even rubbed off
on the rest of the delegation, who were apt to find the New York
taxi drivers surly, to say the least. The British Information Services organization decided to do something about it. They attached to Bevin's person a member of their staff, Bill Ormerod,[4]
who, from long residence in the USA, had acquired up-to-date
public relations techniques. Reminiscent of Bertie Wooster in his
ideas and features, Ormerod was always rushing hotfoot into
Bevin's office full of some new wheeze for winning instant popu-
larity. Bevin did not always find him convincing. He also had difficulty over his name, which he pronounced 'Emeroids'.

One day Ormerod had a more than usually brilliant idea.
Bevin was to go to an important baseball game, then about to
take place in New York. In the interval, his name would be announced over the loudspeakers. Everyone would know he was

---

3 Dixon, *Double Diploma*, p. 241.
4 Sir Berkeley Ormerod, KM, Director, Public Relations, British Information
Services, NY, 1945–62.

there. The news would soon spread throughout New York and Bevin would be acknowledged as a 'regular guy' who liked sport, instead of being regarded merely as a sinister anti-Semitic, political figure.

It was all arranged accordingly. Bevin went to the ball game and the announcement was made. The only drawback was that the crowd, upon hearing over the public-address system that they had 'the good fortune to have present the Right Honourable Ernest Bevin', did not react in the way Ormerod had foretold. On the contrary, they hissed and booed for five minutes. Bevin came away from the ground under heavy escort and with his tail very much between his legs. 'This feller Emeroids,' he muttered on getting back to the safety of his office, 'he's always doing this sort of thing to me.'

However, that was not the end of the story. Bertie Wooster remained undaunted. It seemed that nothing could affect his optimism; and on this occasion, to be sure, he was vindicated. The report of the ball game did indeed spread: news not merely of Bevin's attendance, but of the hostile reception by the New York crowd. This provoked editorial articles saying that whatever might be thought of Bevin's Palestine policy, this was no way to treat a distinguished guest in the hospitable city of New York. There was an upsurge of pro-Bevin feeling. He had faced the mob and been battered. All honour to his courage.

Some time later I heard that Ormerod had been knighted for his services. This struck me as some sort of bow to the principal part played by Providence in public affairs, as well as being a tribute to a particularly debonair punter. I could not but hope also that some of the glory would be reflected upon whoever the Jeeves was in the background.

During the UN Assembly, Bevin went to Washington one weekend. He stayed in the British residence with Archie Clark Kerr, Lord Inverchapel, who was later to be my first ambassador when I was transferred to Washington as Third Secretary the following year. A man of great charm – tweedy and pipe-smoking with the weatherbeaten face of a sheep-farmer – he appealed to politicians by his informality, and, let it be admitted, by his skilfully concealed flattery. Bevin had met him on a visit to Moscow which would normally have been his last post. There, so Bob Dixon told me afterwards, he laid himself out to charm Bevin. He was attentive to Bevin's personal needs, without being at all fussy. He showed that he had no fuddy-duddy prejudice against Labour. By walking about the Moscow residence stripped to the waist and pointing out the garden which he had dug with his own hands, he revealed how fit he was. From the way he talked to the Russians, and their reaction to him, he left no one in any doubt that foreigners found him difficult to resist personally and that he might conceivably get something out of a foreign government for nothing, which could be useful. Bevin appointed him to succeed Halifax in Washington.

In a long career abroad he had become so bored with small talk and polite responses that he longed only for the unusual and unexpected. He would say things in order to shock and so to produce some non-automatic reaction, a temptation he found irresistible in Washington's Victorian society. He adored new ideas – the latest in painting and books, or rather what he thought were the latest, though in practice, having lived abroad so long, he was often a generation behind the times. He loved the young. He gave a party one evening to which he only invited young people. There

I met for the first time the Kennedy clan, including Jack who had recently been elected to Congress. Clark Kerr made us all play 'The Game', then in fashion. We all threw ourselves into it, partly because it was fun and the Kennedys liked games, partly to please the host. The Kennedys did not, I think, find it odd that they should have been invited to the British Embassy for what amounted to a children's party.

Inverchapel ceased to fill the bill as ambassador when the brunt of the work began to touch on economics, of which he knew little, but for a year or two he did indeed get something for nothing out of Washington. Although very much not a public figure, he was a very important private one in Washington in those early years after the war, and succeeded in winning the affection and confidence of many of the key men in the US administration.

Probably the most important event during Bevin's weekend in Washington with Inverchapel was his call on the President. Bevin showed no acrimony when Truman took the initiative in raising the subject of Palestine, although he had been bitter at the President's continued public insistence on the need to admit a large number of Jewish refugees immediately. In response to Bevin's request, Truman undertook to do something about permitting more Jewish immigrants from Europe into the USA. Mr Truman agreed with Bevin's remark that Dr Weizmann was the most intelligent of the Jewish leaders. Nor did he dissent when Bevin said that 'the Jews somehow expect one to fulfil all the prophecies of all the prophets; I tell them sometimes that I can no more fulfil all the prophecies of Ezekiel than I can those of that other great Jew, Karl Marx.' In reporting this remark I must not leave any impression that Bevin was anti-Semitic. In my experience he became increasingly anti-Zionist because he did not believe that the creation of Israel would solve the refugee problem and he knew that it would cause great difficulties with the Arabs for Britain, which had the Mandate for Palestine; but he was never anti-Semitic.

But to return to the meeting with the President. After they had gone round the world together – Palestine, Egypt, India, Indonesia, Germany and the Soviet Union – they talked about their hours of work. The President rose regularly at 5.30 a. m. and was at his desk working at papers till breakfast. He was not usually through until midnight. The previous evening they had had a small celebration in honour of the calling-off of the coal strike, so he had got to bed much later. Yes, there were a great many papers to read and sign every day. Although he had plenty of experts he liked to read things for himself. Bevin said he also had to work before breakfast. About the mass of paperwork he recalled a story about some old colleague, Tom Mann. After being away for a holiday and returning to find a great arrear of correspondence, Tom Mann threw the letters into the fire, saying of the correspondents: 'Those which don't matter have received their answer, those which do, well, they'll write again.'

Truman asked Bevin for a signed photograph. He pointed to the gallery of photographs round the room. The King, General Chiang Kai-chek, Marshal Stalin, Mr Attlee and the Emperor of Abyssinia. The President spoke of his mother whose portrait hung on the wall. She was ninety-four and knew as much as he did about what was going on in the world. Her sight had gone. She relied on the radio. He told how he had flown down to see her recently. What a change between the pace of travel now and in the old days! In reminiscent mood he recalled how forty-odd years ago he had been cutting corn in Missouri. 'At that time,' the Secretary of State said, 'I was selling mineral water.' They both reflected an instant upon the mysterious workings of Providence.

On transfer to Washington in March 1947, I left Bevin's Private Office. I kept in touch with him on and off and when his resignation was announced on 9 March 1951, I was back in London and asked the Private Office if I might see him for a minute to say goodbye.

The following day, Saturday, was his last day in the Office. Herbert Morrison would be coming in on the Monday. I was summoned to the Private Office at about 1.20 p.m. When I went through the swing baize door into his room he was sitting as usual behind the large desk looking straight ahead. He half turned and said 'Hullo, Nicko.' He held his hand out limply and I took it but feared to shake it in case I should hurt him, so frail did he seem. I was struck by how ill and feeble he looked, so much worse than two years previously in Washington, when I last had the chance of talking to him at any length. (He had been there for the signing of the North Atlantic Treaty.)

'I wanted to have the chance of saying goodbye,' I said. 'I am so sorry you are going.'

'Yes, I know,' he said in a friendly way, but very quietly. 'Six years is a long time, and you know I don't know if I've succeeded.'

I was struck by his doubts. When I had seen a lot of him in earlier days he had never admitted to any failure or to qualms about the rightness of what he was doing. But now he was talking almost introspectively. I noticed how immovable his lower lip seemed; it jutted out, dark in colour, as if the blood was clotted inside. His face was much thinner, and the lines of his forehead more sharply delineated; the only thing the same was the streaked black and white hair that, I had always thought, made his head look from behind like a giant bull's-eye.

'I think it has been successful, very successful,' I replied in a matter-of-fact way.

'Well, not altogether,' he said. 'If only I had had a bit longer. But then I don't know if you can ever settle with the Russians.'

'No, you can never settle,' I said, emphasizing the last word. 'But I don't think there'll be war. Do you?'

'No, there won't be war,' Bevin replied slowly and stolidly. 'If only', he went on, 'I'd had time to make the Atlantic Pac' [he always said the word as though it were spelt without a 't'] into something large, into a wider organism, with a budget and other things for the whole area' – he was talking more in his old way now, great, vague but visionary ideas. This time though there was a note of resignation in his voice, as if he realized that he would never be able to carry them out. He sat with his hands lying lifeless on their sides on the desk. He was not smoking, but I noticed from a glass beside him that he had had a drink. I stood looking down on him with my arms folded.

He went on: 'And, given time, I think I would have been able to settle Egypt. I am just on the verge. When we began six years ago nobody knew all the changes that would happen in the Far East. I think without Indonesia I could have done a lot in Asia. I was trying to get down there and then that Indonesian business happened.'

I asked him about his health. 'Oh, it's not too bad, thank you, but on a day like this I don't feel too good.'

He began rubbing his chest over his heart just as he had always done. I might have been back four years, so vividly did I recall the many times I had stood there watching him overcome pain and frailty to tackle some foreign visitor or go over to the House of Commons for a speech.

I could not help saying: 'But you know you often didn't feel well years ago; and you've managed to stick it for so long; it's not bad.'

'No, I suppose not.'

There was a transition here that I do not recall. But he began denouncing Churchill in a way that suggested to me that the widespread call for his resignation had been heightened by something that Churchill had said.

'You know, they never showed me the papers. If they had, I'd have realized the public's reaction and dealt with it so you'd have heard no more about it. As it is, Churchill gets hold of it ...'

As he mentioned Churchill there was a flash of the old indignation, but you felt there was no longer the power behind it. I noticed he no longer chewed the inside of his left cheek, a tic that used to be a favourite accompaniment to wrath or rumination.

'You know,' he said, suddenly chuckling to himself, as he used to do, though without the habitual shaking, 'of all the times we've wandered about together in different places, and at all those conferences, the time I remember you best was when we went out on the doctor's ship. I always think of you there on deck. We had a good time, didn't we?'

'Yes.'

Naturally I remembered the occasion vividly. Bevin went on:

'I was only talking the other day to the doctor about that time on the ship. And I said that when I retired we must do it again, and that we would have Nicko down.' He turned to me and laughed aloud, moving his big hand to his knee.

'Yes, I'd love to,' I said. 'If you ever want any help writing about your first years as Foreign Secretary, I'd love to help you.'

'Thank you, I'll take advantage of that. But I must let a month or two pass to get away from it a bit.'

'Yes, I understand. You'll remain in touch with foreign affairs though, I suppose?'

'Oh yes. You see, I'll be on the Defence Committee as well as in the Cabinet, but I must take it easy for a bit.'

Bevin seemed to be getting very tired. It was about 1.45 p.m. by this time and no doubt he'd had a long morning. He got up gingerly from his chair. I noticed he had been sitting on an air cushion. He held his hand out for me to shake it. I did so and he moved slowly towards the cloakroom.

'Give my wishes to your father,' he said. (They had participated together on the Macmillan Committee.)

I retreated to the Private Office very much hoping that this was not the last time I would see him. A few minutes later I saw him drive away from the Park Door entrance to the Foreign Office. I knew that he would be minding the break, but I also knew that he would be unsentimental about it. He managed to inspire personal affection without being sentimental. As his car made away, I thought how completely without self-pity he was – in spite of his stab-in-the-back speeches – and how, although egotistical, he was not vain. I do not think that he thought about his place in history – at least I never heard him mention it – though I do not believe that he would have been surprised about the judgement by Alan Bullock, not a historian given to hyperbole: 'Bevin seems to me to belong to that small group of men who can be said to have had a decisive impact on the history of their time.'[5]

I never saw him again, but such was the pull of his personality that when, a few weeks later, I read of his death one evening, on the Reuters tape, I hurried, without thinking, to his flat at No. 1 Carlton Gardens, where he had continued to live after giving up the Foreign Office. Neither the policemen nor the porter knew me, and they were rather suspicious of my intentions, not surprisingly because I was not sure of them myself. I asked for Bevin's detective, Ben Macey, and was told, 'Oh, he's gone off, of course, now.' That certainly seemed to sum up the finality of Bevin's death, and thinking of him I walked away disconsolately. His capacity for winning loyalty and affection from those who worked most closely with him – singled out by Attlee as his outstanding characteristic – made his loss the greater as it also heightened the gain of those who had had the chance of knowing and serving him.

---

5 Bullock, *Ernest Bevin*, Vol. III, p. 857.

5

MY SECOND SPELL IN THE PRIVATE OFFICE

When Sir Alec Douglas-Home succeeded Mr Harold Macmillan as Prime Minister in October 1963, Mr R. A. Butler was made Foreign Secretary and I was appointed his Principal Private Secretary in succession to Oliver Wright,[1] who accompanied Douglas-Home to No. 10. In the sixteen years since I had last been in the Private Office I had served in Washington, Athens, Vienna and Santiago and I was Head of the Northern Department of the FO when summoned to serve Rab.

Early the following year the Prime Minister, accompanied by Lady Home, visited Washington. The Foreign Secretary was included in the party, as was Mrs Butler. I tagged along behind them.

A special Comet was made available for the journey. Its range was inadequate for east-west Atlantic crossings in winter, and the journey took us a long time. It enabled me to observe how easily

---

1 Sir Oliver Wright, diplomat. Later Ambassador to Copenhagen, Bonn and Washington.

Home applied himself to the work which he had set aside for the plane. He first prepared the speech he was to make at Toronto, scribbling notes with a biro on a small pad of Basildon Bond writing paper. Then he tackled the enormous pile of briefs for the Washington talks. There were over forty of them. He went at them with no fuss, and without even the aid of a cigarette or a drink. Lady Home sat beside him. She did not chat. She wrote letters. She knitted. The two of them made as unassuming a couple as you could have seen anywhere.

Meanwhile the Private Secretaries from No. 10 went about their tasks in their own way. There was much shuffling of papers, and occasionally a shorthand typist would be summoned from the back of the plane. Those invited to lunch at the front of the plane, in the VIP section, would be notified. It was very much a No. 10 show, though the Private Secretaries did allow temporarily into the magic circle the Secretary of the Cabinet, Sir Burke Trend, a quiet, tolerant, don-like figure who wore with great and natural modesty the inevitable influence he always had with the Prime Minister of the day. The Butlers sat the other side of the gangway from the Homes, and I tried to see that they were properly looked after, though from the moment of take-off they must have had the feeling of being slightly out of it, which is common to all Foreign Secretaries travelling in the shadow of the PM. It must be added, however, that the Homes did their best to offset this throughout the journey without being in any way patronizing.

We broke the journey at Ottawa for talks with the Canadian Government. We stayed at Government House with the Governor-General, Georges Vanier, a French-Canadian who seemed to combine in his person some of the best qualities of French and North American civilization. It was cold, bright, winter weather. The snow was thick upon the lawns and lay puckered up like a blanket round the enormous conservatory which led off from the house. The plants, flowers and seedlings, flourishing in the brilliant sun and the steam heating of the greenhouse, took on the enhanced value of incongruity in the midst of the winter landscape. I spent much time there the first morning before going into breakfast – a large, communal affair, reminiscent of a country-house party before some great sporting event.

This seemed the perfect setting for the PM. Breakfast parties, I recalled, having just read a life of Monckton Milnes, were part of the tradition of aristocratic public life. Seated at the large mahogany table with an enfilade of toast-racks, Alec Home looked very much at home as he shook out the cornflakes. Newspapers lay about the room, but the outside world was kept in its place. There must be a time for everything. A large grandfather clock ticked reassuringly. The talk – light-hearted and general – was about clocks, skating, birds and open-air life, while everyone helped themselves to coffee and bacon and eggs and, if so moved, to devilled kidneys, which stood upon the hotplates on the sideboard. Neither public affairs, nor shop of any kind, was ever mentioned. It seemed an unwarranted intrusion when eventually a butler shimmered in to announce that the car was at the door to take Sir Alec to fulfil his appointment with the Canadian Prime Minister. The idyll was shattered. As so often in travel, nothing else about that visit to North America quite came up to this first moment, before the real purpose had begun, unless it be the recollection of it.

In Washington the visit repeated the pattern of so many ministerial meetings: the principals on each side made statements on
all outstanding problems, speaking from papers prepared by their
officials and containing little that was not familiar to the officials
on the other side, who in turn had of course briefed their political masters. Though a general aura of goodwill was created, nothing of substance was altered in policy or attitudes. True, some
months later, soon after Labour had been returned to office, a
ministerial visit to Washington did actually make a difference in
certain respects. For a long time the US Government had been
urging their Western European allies to accept the idea of a multilateral force (MLF) to meet Federal Germany's claim to have
some say in the handling and control of nuclear weapons. In
Britain there was scepticism in both main political parties about
the value of the whole scheme, and when Harold Wilson, accompanied by Gordon Walker, went to Washington soon after the October 1964 election, they left the President, Rusk, Macnamara,
and George Ball in no doubt about their opposition to the MLR
L. B. J. listened. He listened silently for a long time doing a samba
backwards and forwards in his anglepoise chair. He hardly spoke,
to the British delegation at any rate, though he carried out whispered consultations behind the back of his hand with his own
Ministers. However, from the time of that meeting, we never
heard anything more about US insistence on the MLR L. B. J.
killed it at that conference.

During this Wilson visit something else occurred which was
outside the scope of normal diplomatic channels. The US Ministers made moving appeals to their British colleagues not to aban-
don their role in the Far East. Concerned over Britain's balance of

payments difficulties, they were afraid that the Labour Government would suddenly do in the Far East what they had done in Greece in 1947, pull out and leave the burden of resisting the spread of Communism entirely to the USA. Rusk said with some eloquence and evident sincerity that the US did not want to be left alone with the task of maintaining peace in the Far East, and that they were convinced that Britain still had an important role there. I had the impression that this appeal had an effect, unacknowledged at the time, which endured until our economic difficulties became still more acute a few years later.

However, on the occasion of the February 1964 Home-Butler visit to Washington, when elections were on the horizon in both countries, it would have been unrealistic to have expected anything very important or lasting to have occurred. Home and Butler spoke from their prepared briefs. Rusk replied in his customary matter-of-fact vein. L. B. J. rocked and showed little interest. He invariably looked extremely bored until some secretary came in to tell him that a member of Congress was anxious to see him, upon which his spirits rose visibly and, apologizing with little conviction, he left the meeting.

Rab was fascinated to watch a high-powered US politician at close quarters. He thought him less like the chairman of the Conservative Party than like the chairman of the National Farmers' Union. He was intrigued by his social graces; by his habit of handing out autographs unsolicited. During lunch at the British Embassy, L. B. J., who was seated next to Mrs Butler, gave her five autographs. He just grabbed anything available – his place card, the menu, or a box of matches – signed his name and handed it over.

Travel with Rab had its own peculiar flavour. He did not appear to enjoy it much, though he was prepared to undergo it for a number of motives, some of which were unmixed, Mrs Butler's enthusiasm for one. She liked it in the same way as most people like a break from routine, their friends and the English climate. But she also liked the appurtenances of VIP travel: the special aircraft, the bouquets, the banquets, and of course the frequent Press Conferences at which Rab could show his paces. To us in the Private Office she showed all this with disarming naturalness. She often told us how much she envied us our luck in being able to look forward to hundreds more lovely, lovely journeys even if the beastly Socialists were returned to power. To foreigners Mrs Butler manifested warmth and gratitude. She did so with that plenitude of gesture which the English, contrary to their reputation for reserve, are inclined to display abroad, as though, by violent movement of the forearm, they hope to overcome the tongue-tying inhibitions of a foreign language. Subconsciously, the very generosity of Mrs Butler's response may have owed something to the economy of his. Rab was smiling but unforthcoming in his reaction to hospitality abroad. He was apt to look decidedly bored.

His attitude to 'abroad' was equivocal. He was curious, he was amused, he was not patronizing. He was invariably courteous, particularly, it must be said, if the foreigners showed English traits. The Office managed to get him to take much more interest in some Latin-American official of the UN who was to play a part in Cyprus by explaining that he was a scratch golfer.

He was uncannily observant. Con O'Neill[2] gave a lunch for

2 Sir Con O'Neill, diplomat. At this time British Ambassador to the European Communities.

him in Brussels one day to enable him to meet some of the representatives to the EEC and the members of the Commission. There must have been about fifteen guests. Rab sat in the middle of the table. I was at one end. Beside me sat the Italian representative. After the party was over and we were driving away, Rab, in between random comments on the names and descriptions on the shop-fronts which he read out as we passed, said:

'What a lot the Italian ate.'

'Which do you mean?' I asked, thinking that he could not possibly have seen as far down the table as my neighbour.

'There was only one Italian,' he replied, 'the man next to you. Did you not see how he took three rolls, and never stopped eating the whole way through lunch?'

'No,' I confessed, 'I didn't notice.'

'Oh, I always watch these things.'

It reminded me of a remark he had made earlier about liking to go out to dinner in London. He had explained that dinner parties enabled him to pick up important information about people which he could not get sitting in an office. 'Wives talk,' he said. 'I get a lot of information from them.' He went on to describe how, from one such source, he knew the exact medical state of one of his colleagues who had been ill, though the Minister himself had said nothing about it. Ann Fleming told me once that she loved sitting next to Rab at dinner because he was so immensely indiscreet and told her all about the other Ministers. So the disclosure of information appears to have been two-way.

Rab was intrigued by foreign languages. Returning by air from Germany after some visit, he spent the whole journey reading a German newspaper from cover to cover, including all the advertisements. However, he was inclined to look at foreign problems through very British eyes, and to consider them of interest largely in relation to their bearing on our affairs. There was something Anglo-Indian in his approach, which was not surprising, given his background. Abroad was not really his milieu, and he could sometimes look out of place. He looked particularly out of place in Japan.

We travelled there via Washington where Rab had to attend one of the periodic meetings of CENTO.[3] It was always very agreeable staying with the Ormsby-Gores,[4] who managed somehow to be rather grand without being in the slightest bit pompous. Sissy was pretty, unstuffy, shy and alive. David had had the entrée to the White House under President Kennedy and to the whole Kennedy clan, which had given him a unique position in Washington until Dallas. He struggled on afterwards applying his highly attuned political ear to the rapidly changing London-Washington relationship, but naturally it could never be quite the same again.

The visit provided the opportunity for some private talk between Rab and Rusk.[5] Rab had the capacity for winning confidences out of people, despite his reputation for indiscretion. He was a good listener, and knew the weaknesses of human nature. He was not at all overbearing as a personality. He was what the Spaniards call *simpático*. Rusk told him of some of his personal

---

3 Central Treaty Organization, formed in 1955 for the defence of the Middle East.
4 David Ormsby-Gore, later Lord Harlech, British Ambassador to Washington 1961–5. His first wife Sylvia died in 1967.
5 Dean Rusk, US Secretary of State 1961–9.

problems as Secretary of State, including the financial sacrifice involved. He had little domestic help at home, and his wife had to do the cooking. He indicated that he welcomed the chance for a completely off-the-record chat with someone like Rab, who had like himself no axe to grind.

Some of this explains Rusk's success as Secretary of State, and, judged at any rate by one important criterion, he was a success in a way John Foster Dulles[6] was not. I am not talking about the shaping and direction of US foreign policy, but about the general impact of the US government on the governments of foreign countries; about the kind of first impression created on foreign ministries all over the world and the instantaneous reactions produced. Here Rusk managed, despite the extremely unpromising background of the Vietnam War, which dominated so much of his term of office, to create an impression favourable to the USA. He was the ideal sort of person for the US government to have at a time when they were engaged in highly unpopular military operations. For no one could ever have suspected him of aggressive tendencies. He had no bombast. He was very unassuming personally. He was no orator. He was completely disinterested personally, and no other Foreign Secretary could possibly have feared that Rusk was trying to claim the personal credit for anything. He didn't try to score off anyone. He stated the US government's point of view with complete matter-of-factness. There were humanity and compassion and reason in what he said, but no heroics or emotion. He was anxious that everyone should understand what the US government were doing, and were prepared

---

6 John Foster Dulles, US Secretary of State 1953–9.

to do, and their motives. These he explained with great patience, so that foreign governments should have no sense that the US government were trying to browbeat them against their will. If there was little sense of occasion and no attempt to dramatize anything, the temperature was always kept low, which is where it should be in international gatherings. Rusk did not strike a great figure personally at the many meetings I attended, but this made him all the more appropriate and effective as the representative of the most powerful country.

However, apart from the friendly exchanges between Rusk and Rab which took place on the side-lines of this CENTO meeting in the spring of 1964, the visit to Washington was not a great success from the British standpoint. This was partly because Rab, very uncharacteristically, mishandled his Press Conference; he gave it at the beginning rather than at the end of his visit, and blurted out something about the United Arab Republic[7] producing atomic weapons. He left Washington in a cloud of uncontradicted speculation which included graphic accounts of the rebuff President Johnson was said to have given him over Cuba. From the new Dulles airport, which to our old-world eyes seemed like a scene from science fiction, we flew westwards into the evening sun which held aloft almost interminably, prolonging our day till we were all wilting.

Upon arrival at Honolulu at midnight we awakened ourselves with a bathe. Michael Hadow, the Head of the News Department, was the most entertaining of travelling companions, seeking and

---

7 The UAR, a political union created between Egypt and Syria in 1958. Syria seceded in 1961.

finding the best and worst in the passing scene, beginning every journey, no matter the time or place, with a gin and tonic and *The Times* crossword and finishing off both with aplomb. He was an integral part of the Private Office touring team. Rab was fascinated by Michael's life-style. 'I suppose', he gurgled to me one day, 'he could not keep up with the Press in any other way.'

The following morning Michael and I compared notes on the garlands of frangipani, the trolley of fresh pineapples and the coconut waffle-cakes that had been wheeled into our rooms for breakfast. We joined the girls for a swim and sunbathe. We watched travel-ad-looking men surfing. In keeping with the mood I bought a comic postcard and sent it off to Ian Fleming (who had just named a particularly nasty character in his latest novel after me). Then back to the plane for a ten-hour flight to Tokyo. Michael and I were served planter's punches and 'hot oriental snacks', as the BAC menu described them. The Butlers managed to turn the bar into their private compartment. Rab flicked the pages of a book, showed some interest in the boxes and dozed. Mrs Butler talked to Tom Bridges about modern poetry, particularly Rupert Brooke. Tom was an appropriate audience because he was the grandson of the former Poet Laureate. He was also a model Private Secretary. I recall him saying to someone who consulted him about how to achieve advancement in the public service that he should take great care with his drafting and never draft for himself but for the signature of others. In this respect he reminded me of Machiavelli's words in *The Prince*, though Tom is the least Machiavellian of men: 'When you see that the adviser thinks more about himself than about you, and that in all his deeds he seeks his own self-interest, such a man as this will never be a good adviser and you will never be able to trust him.' Such has been the trust that people have placed in Tom Bridges that he has had a distinguished career and is now British Ambassador to Rome.

We reached Tokyo in thick mist and heavy rain, to be greeted by a tarmac-ful of journalists and photographers, each with an umbrella. We had been putting our clocks back hour after hour – except Rab, who insisted on leaving his at London time – so that by now, when our eyes fell upon this oriental Renoir they were already drooping. However, before we could go to bed there was a little dinner at the British residence. The Ambassadress valiantly did her best to keep us awake with lively conversational gambits, of which one, geared to the guest of honour, went, 'I do so hate progress. Don't you?' In point of fact Rab was invariably on the side of progress, but he did not quite have the strength to take up the challenge just then.

For the visitor there is a good yardstick by which to gauge in advance the hospitality likely to be found in a British embassy residence: the simple one of the market-place. The greater the traffic, the more the boredom created by, and the less the attention paid to, each guest. Japan was sufficiently far away from London to avoid being sated. Besides which the residence had the claim of being a very British house, like that of an Edwardian headmaster or bishop, set in a compound in the middle of a very strange city.

During the meetings with the Japanese Foreign Minister and his delegation, Rab was at his most impressionistic. There was nothing over-definite about his brushwork. I was reminded of how he had told me once that during his time as FO spokesman in the House of Commons before the war he had developed a technique of saying quite a lot without anyone afterwards being able to pin anything on him. The Japanese listened smiling and inscrutable while the interpreter made the best of a hard job. Afterwards I knew there would be a moment of truth and they would come, imploring and bewildered, to ask me to clarify first one point, then another, and finally – yes, if you don't mind, if you would be so kind – the whole of Mr Butler's most interesting statement.

It was a mistake of our Embassy, though they could scarcely be expected to know it, to insist upon Rab's paying a visit outside Tokyo to Japan's elder statesman, Yoshida, then over eighty. I do not think elder statesmen like each other as a rule. Rab was already entering their lists, but the real reason for his lack of enthusiasm was that he belonged to the generation of British politicians which had served under Churchill when he hung on as PM in his eighties after he had ceased to be up to the job. On Sunday morning we drove the forty miles, much of it through the outskirts of Tokyo, to Oiso, for lunch with Yoshida, a journey only made possible by the intervention of motor-cycle outriders who, with a perpetual banshee wail, cut a swathe through the dense traffic. As the Rolls swept along, Rab repeatedly asked himself, his wife Mollie and me, in so far as the noise permitted, whether it was really true that this octogenarian was the most important person for him to visit out of the whole hundred million Japanese, a doubt not entirely dispelled when he was greeted on arrival by a troop of schoolgirls in girl-guide costume standing at the ready at the bottom of Yoshida's beautiful Japanese garden.

Yoshida and his daughter were most hospitable. We had a

delicious lunch during which Mrs Butler was presented with a handbag. Afterwards we sat in the conservatory amidst exotic plants. Mrs Butler did her best to keep the conversation going cheerfully. Rab looked like a Buddha. In the afternoon they drove straight back to Tokyo. Ted Peck[8] and I went with Yoshida's daughter to the mountains, a beautiful drive which came to an abrupt end on our return journey about twenty-five miles from the centre of Tokyo when we were completely ensnarled in traffic. We eventually got back by train. My overriding impression from the visit to Tokyo was the density of population and the scarcity of trees which made London seem like Rus in Urbe by comparison.

Before leaving Tokyo I took part in a scene that should really have belonged to one of those Whitehall farces that were so popular at the time. In the planning for departure it was agreed that all our luggage had to be packed up and sent off to the aeroplane early in the morning of the day we were flying. I had left myself with a tropical suit to wear without realizing that the trousers had several flybuttons missing. I put it on but found the gap too wide for decency. Meanwhile my pyjamas and dressing-gown had gone with my luggage to the airport. Problem: how was I going to get fly-buttons sewn on? Without thinking it out thoroughly I rang the bell. A Japanese servant-woman entered and bowed. I was sitting on my bed. I pointed to my flies. Impassive but polite she bowed lower, stayed there a moment and then withdrew from the room backwards. I was wondering feebly what to do next when

---

8 Sir Edward Peck, diplomat, Assistant Under-Secretary of State, Foreign Office, later British Representative to NATO.

she returned with another Japanese maid. 'Ah,' I thought, 'she presumably speaks English.' But not at all. The two of them looked at me silently and bent double. Again I pointed at myself, then at the door and did a mime hoping to indicate: 'Now if you will just withdraw I'll slip off my trousers and pass them to you round the door.' But not surprisingly they did not understand and retreated from the room with the same backward shuffle. The scene was undergoing a third performance with yet another servant in the company, when the Ambassadress appeared and, with skilful interpretation, put things right. The Ambassador explained to me afterwards that the Japanese are used to the eccentric habits of the English abroad, but they don't usually expect them to misbehave so early in the morning.

We flew back via the Philippines, and as we took off from Okinawa for Manila I had to ask myself whether it could really be true that we were going there. For months the Office had been trying to persuade Rab to include a call on President Macapagal of the Philippines in his return journey from Japan. They hoped that it would be useful in getting his support for some move over the Malaysia-Indonesia confrontation, but Rab had prevaricated.

'I'll only be able to touch the fringe of the subject,' he protested at an Office meeting; 'and it'll be hot.'

There was silence amongst the officials. Sensing disapproval, Rab went on: 'But I'm tough. I'm much tougher than I look. I wouldn't have been in politics that long if I hadn't been pretty tough. But my political nose tells me that it would be wrong to go. Of course, if you say it's my duty, then I'll go.'

He did not want to agree to the inclusion of Manila in the itinerary; on the other hand, he wanted the possibility left open. It emerged later that Mrs Butler was giving a 21st birthday party for her eldest son on the day after we were due back. A call at Manila would add greatly to her tiredness, though as Rab told yet another Office meeting called to discuss this hardy theme: 'Of course, women must have second, and public duty first place.'

But still he resisted a commitment either way. 'I don't want to die in the Pacific,' he said pathetically one morning. After still further Office pressure on the subject, in which Harold Caccia[9] had been involved, he confided to Tom Bridges and me: 'I could see Harold's face all puckered up when I said I might not go to Manila. Why do you think he minds? There's nothing in it for him.' We muttered something a little sententious about disinterested advice.

Doggedness on our part and frequent appeals to the public interest succeeded in the end. And there we now were, airborne for the Philippines. We only stayed about twenty-four hours there, but both Mr and Mrs Butler decided to make the most of them. It was difficult to know why their mood was so elated suddenly, unless it was because they had their noses set for home. But they paid calls, attended banquets and went sightseeing with great gusto and without any complaints about the heat. Such a success were they that at the end of the visit President Macapagal was readier than he had been at the outset to take some initiative with Sukarno over confrontation.

The heat exacerbated a personal problem for me. In Tokyo, Yoshida's daughter had entrusted to me, for delivery to friends in

---

9 Lord Caccia, diplomat, British Ambassador to Austria and the USA. Permanent Under-Secretary of State, Foreign Office, 1962–5.

England, a box of partridge eggs for hatching. They had to be kept at an even temperature throughout the journey, yet they must not be put on ice. I decided to keep them more or less on my person, on the principle that, if I could survive, so could the eggs. This meant that when I accompanied the Foreign Secretary to his various meetings in Manila, I was laden, not merely with the usual box of papers, but with this mysterious parcel which would sit beside me on the seat, to the surprise of the otherwise carefree Filipinos listening anxiously for the tick. It seemed too difficult to explain, and too frivolous to introduce myself, on arrival at the office of the President for instance, by giving my name and then saying 'and this is a box of partridge eggs from Japan'.

We stayed in Manila with the Ambassador, John Addis, whom I have already described in his misery at Chequers. Here he was in his element. As we breakfasted together in his garden he told me how delighted he was with Manila. His passion was fourteenth-century blue China porcelain. He revealed to me with a glint in his eye that recently some ruins had been discovered in the Philippines with Chinese pots in them. He showed me an article he had just written for some learned journal on gourd designs on early Chinese pottery. I caught his enthusiasm as I basked in the early morning sun, a sense of well-being heightened, to be sure, by the delicious mangoes I was eating. Later I told the Foreign Secretary about the mangoes. I enthused on their uncanny taste to Mrs Butler. I made Tom Bridges view them with an open mind. Finally, I arranged to steal a moment out of the day to go to the fruit market and buy dozens of them to distribute to the other members of the Private Office on return.

Such was my euphoria over the visit that I had no difficulty, before we left, in dictating a glowing communiqué on the success of the Butlers' stay in Manila. Less easy was the task of struggling on to the plane carrying papers, and of course partridge eggs, and now also a basket of mangoes.

We travelled back via Bangkok, New Delhi, Teheran and Beirut – to us little more than a succession of hot and unchanging VIP lounges, though at Teheran I managed at 2 a.m. to buy Mary, my wife, an antique slave bracelet, which she has worn ever since.

It was always a relief to get back to the plane and to fasten our seat-belts to the delicious smell of the fruit. This arrived back safely and was shared out as planned. As for the partridge eggs these were handed over to the prescribed destination, though I did not know who the actual beneficiary was. I did not therefore find out whether that particular mission had succeeded or not, an uncertainty that induced in me certain Ancient Mariner feelings. It was only some twenty years later when I happened to be talking to Sir William Keswick and, the conversation turning to the Far East and to exotic birds, I mentioned my role as egg-courier, that I was enlightened. Sir William said he was pleased to be able to thank me however belatedly and to assure me that most of the eggs had hatched. I must say that I felt a sense of relief; the impact of our visit on Japan two decades ago had been fleeting, and it was consoling to know that something more permanent had been achieved by the introduction of these Japanese partridges into Scotland.

6

THE TOOLS OF THE TRADE; RAB AT WORK

As painters employ brush and palette, doctors stethoscope and thermometer, barristers brief and wig, so Foreign Secretaries rely upon telegrams and speeches as indispensable tools of their trade.

In my two spells in the Private Office, the day would begin with uniformed office-keepers bearing in flat boxes of telegrams. These, I believe, have given place to newfangled methods of delivery which diminish the aura but not the content. It is the task of the most junior Private Secretary to put the telegrams into some sort of order whether of geography or priority. I was doing this one morning when I had just joined the Private Office and was still a completely new boy to the Service. There was no one else in the room. Suddenly Gladwyn Jebb[1] burst in. He looked around a moment, strolled up and down and then declared, head in air, 'There does not seem to be anybody here,' before sweeping

---

1 Lord Gladwyn, diplomat, served in various posts at home and abroad including that of Ambassador to Paris from 1954 to 1960.

out. Later I came to be less disconcerted by Gladwyn's grand manner, particularly when I saw it deployed as loftily towards the important as the unimportant.

Despite all the new media of communication, the telegrams retain their hold upon all those privileged to have access to them; they appear to meet a deep-seated human desire for secret communication (satisfied in childhood by means of invisible ink). They are the sources of information not vouchsafed to the world at large; and the outward telegrams bear the Foreign Secretary's instructions on every important issue affecting British interests.

'No more boxes' (of telegrams) was the immediate cry of Sir Winston Churchill when he finally realized that he had lost the 1945 election, according to a visitor who saw him at the precise moment.[2] It was the same with Rab. On his last morning in the Foreign Secretary's room after the 1964 general election, when he knew he would be unlikely ever to hold office again, he spoke sadly of how much he would miss the telegrams.

Yet they can be an awful drag, and those left unread during the day, which are often numerous, can be the last straw that makes the overnight box unbearable. Describing the boxes as 'the bane of every Foreign Secretary's life', Alan Bullock relates how Bevin, who hardly ever looked at a book, would get up regularly at 5 a.m. to read them right through.[3] Michael Stewart, most dutiful of Ministers, said once in his quiet way when a discussion was going on between officials in his room about putting some telegrams in his box for the night: 'You know, I sometimes wonder what the

2 Colonel Sir Charles Ponsonby, *Ponsonby Remembers*.
3 Bullock, *Ernest Bevin*, Vol. III, p. 99.

R.A. Butler in Downing Street .

Private Secretaries think I do at night.' The sorry tone only made the reproach all the more telling, and for a time the Private Secretaries exercised restraint in making up the box. Michael Stewart wrote, on the basis of his exhausting experience with FO boxes: 'One of the qualifications for Cabinet Office is an ability to do with less than the normal allowance of sleep.'[4] In the chapter of his autobiography dealing with the task of being a Minister, Hugh Dalton has written: 'A golden rule for Ministers is not to read too much.'[5] The same point is made by Mary Agnes Hamilton in her life of Arthur Henderson: 'The danger lying in wait for the conscientious Foreign Secretary is that he may be overwhelmed by ... sheer weight of diversified work, and either sink under red boxes or subside into formal functions.'[6]

It would be easier were the Foreign Secretary not, nowadays, meant to be the last word in information as well as the maker of policy. He rushes about the world, and no sooner has he arrived in a foreign capital than he is asked to give a Press Conference which may touch on any international question. Britain's loss of relative power does not seem to have made world-wide expectations of her Foreign Secretaries' omniscience any less, or reduced the hope that he will say something interesting, and, if possible, indiscreet on any current topic.

Some Secretaries of State are kept awake at night by the boxes with which they are sent home every night by the Private Office; others can hardly sleep without them. Rab was an addict. His wife used to complain that he preferred the 'beastly boxes' to the the-

---

4 Michael Stewart, *Life and Labour*, p. 80.
5 Dalton, *High Tide and After*, p. 19.
6 Mary Agnes Hamilton, *Arthur Henderson: A Biography*, p. 285.

atre or going out to dinner. He dealt with them effortlessly, never wasting time or energy in tinkering with drafts. It was a favourite saying of his that 'paper' had been Herbert Morrison's undoing as Foreign Secretary and that it was only a lifetime spent in Whitehall that had given him the technique to enable him to handle the enormous pile of work the FO inflicted on him nightly. In the middle of an office meeting held one morning to consider some problem raised in telegrams submitted to him in his overnight box, Rab said rhetorically: 'Your Foreign Secretary has mastered the problem, hasn't he?' Then raising his withered right arm he added: 'Despite the boxes of papers so high last night. *Je ne suis pas si bête que j'en ai l'air.*' Needless to say, the last thing anyone in the Office thought Rab to be was *bête*.

But they soon became aware of the characteristics for which he had become famous in Whitehall: inability to make up his mind or confront an issue or a person. They were all brought prominently into play by the Cyprus question that dominated much of Rab's term in office. George Ball, who was the Under-Secretary of State in the USA State Department, was about to come to London for discussions about it. So an Office meeting was agreed, attended by Carrington[7] and Caccia amongst others. It was suggested that the Secretary of State should get together with Duncan Sandys who was Secretary of State for Commonwealth Affairs and was, therefore, directly responsible at that time for Cyprus. I knew from Rab's expression and the way he applied his spectacle case to the end of his nose that he was not going to

---

7 Lord Carrington, at that time Minister without Portfolio and Leader of the House of Lords; later Foreign Secretary (1979–82).

take this hurdle. Looking sideways out of his face and with a slight gurgle he said: 'Well, it's like visiting a friend's farm, isn't it? When you see the bull lying quietly in its pen it seems a pity to kick it and stir it up. Duncan's been quite easy lately, quite reasonable really, hasn't he? And it seems a pity to wake him up.'

Well, George Ball came, without the British Ministers concerned having concerted their line in advance. However, in a long meeting with him attended on the British side by Rab, Duncan Sandys, Carrington and officials from the two departments and, after a working lunch provided by Government Hospitality at No. 1 Carlton Gardens, general agreement was reached about tactics and the ultimate objective, and it was decided that officials from both sides should get together to commit the outcome to writing.

When I reached the Private Office early the following morning, I found the room full of Ministers and officials eager to see Rab immediately. They were waving a memorandum – the document agreed between the officials – and they wanted to get the Foreign Secretary's concurrence immediately because Ball was on the point of flying back to Washington. We went in. Rab read it and then said somewhat grumpily that he had not approved it. He asked one or two oblique questions; he referred to one or two things he did not like about it; he expressed fear that it would leak. Leaving everyone in some disorder, he said he would go over and talk about it with the Prime Minister. He was back in the Foreign Office in no time and immediately reassembled the meeting, saying, 'Well, your Ministers have considered the subject. Alec and Duncan's views are the same as mine, we definitely don't like it, we don't want to have any piece of paper. We think the Americans should do something.'

There was a glum silence until the Permanent Under-Secretary, Caccia, ever practical, and swift as a pike to understand politicians' minds, suggested that we ourselves might use the paper informally as a guide for our own action, and that the immediate need was to agree with the Americans upon instructions to U Thant.[8] Rab was much relieved and, having insisted once again that Ministers were not bound by the paper, that all copies should be numbered and that the utmost secrecy over it must be observed, he went on to other things.

Afterwards Carrington asked me what Rab was up to: 'He agreed with the whole thing the day before. What's happened to make him go back on it all?' I explained that had I been able to see the paper in advance I could have told him that there would not have been the slightest chance of Rab's agreeing. He did not want to be tied down in that sort of way.

One day, leaning back in his chair applying his spectacle case to his nose with one hand and scratching the back of his head with the other, Rab asked me if I knew his favourite character in literature. I shook my head. 'Well it's Marshall Kutuzov in *War and Peace*; I always found him a very attractive character. His attitude in dealing with the French invasion was to delay and withdraw. I think I am rather like him.'

This certainly was Rab's attitude. He never had a head-on collision. He rarely gave a firm or final rejection of anything. He always refrained from shutting the door. 'Keep in touch' was his favourite way of ending some interview or letter – often with disastrous results because the recipient, taking him at his word,

---

8 U Thant, Secretary-General of the UN 1962–71.

would ring up seeking further contact, which was not at all what Rab had in mind.

It has been frequently said that Rab's besetting weakness was his inability to make up his mind, but I do not think that it is adequate to describe him as indecisive. True, in small things, such as whether or not to go to some party, he found it difficult to decide. For example, he was expected to go one evening to a National Day cocktail party at the Moroccan Embassy. He had a dinner afterwards. At about 6 p.m. he looked at me with his head on one side and asked, 'Do you really think I need go to the Moroccans?' 'No,' I replied unhesitatingly; 'there's absolutely no need.'

That was that until he was on the point of leaving the office that evening. As he stepped into the lift Rab said, 'So you really don't think I need go to this party?' 'No; certainly not,' I answered.

About half an hour later the telephone rang. Rab never introduced himself. He assumed that one knew by instinct that it was he. 'I'm in the flat. I just wanted to be sure that there is no need for me to look in on the Moroccans.' I gave him the assurance.

The next morning we asked him whether, as a matter of courtesy, he ought not to write to the Moroccan Ambassador to apologize for unavoidable absence the night before.

'Oh, I went,' he said.

But in bigger matters, not coming to a conclusion about a particular course of action was a positive decision. He did it deliberately and he had often found that he had avoided trouble that way, however much his critics accused him of applying tactics of *reculer pour mieux reculer*. He had acute political antennae so that he was very much alive to anything that might cause difficulties.

One of the consequences of his view about the role of Ministers in government was that he bothered little with drafts. But there was one occasion when he did intervene in a matter of detail that showed his technique. Not long before the 1964 general election, the Foreign Office was under heavy pressure from the Board of Trade to agree to the opening of a line of credit to a particular country. For various reasons the FO did not support the idea and at a meeting held in the Secretary of State's room the official view was accepted and Mr Butler asked that a reply be drafted to the President of the Board of Trade. When the draft was produced and put in his box overnight, Rab minuted on it that the Office had been too zealous; the letter covered too much ground; he preferred to tackle the President of the Board of Trade piecemeal. Asked for a fuller explanation by a somewhat baffled department, Rab said that he did not think a head-on clash with the President was desirable or necessary. He would prefer to reply to him in stages. The draft should confine itself to asking for further information on why it was thought that the country concerned would not increase trade without long-term credit. By the time the Board of Trade had produced an answer on that, the President would be busy in his constituency; and by the time that he, Rab, was ready with a further letter in answer to that, the general election would be in full swing and the whole subject would have become academic. This is how he proceeded to play it, and events followed just as he had predicted. It would be wrong to describe it as an exercise in indecision; a very definite decision had been taken to procrastinate and avoid decision, and considerable legerdemain and persistence were required to carry it to a satisfactory conclusion – from his point of view.

The Private Office is at its most pivotal in the long and

complicated process of preparing the Foreign Secretary's speeches. The departments of the Office regard a forthcoming Ministerial speech as an opportunity for showing HMG's continuing interest in different parts of the world. 'The Secretary of State can't give a review of foreign policy', each protests, 'without mentioning the Middle East/Far East/Latin America/ Europe', as the case may be; and every Head of Department sends in some little bromide for incorporation in the draft. The result of course is ungripping.

Bevin was a most dutiful deliverer of these disjointed clichés – *tours d'horizon*, he proudly called them in his best and only French. The House of Commons listened to them no less dutifully, as he plodded his way around the world, and on occasion when the horizon became a little uncertain owing to his unique rendering of some place name, the Members became quite interested. His introduction of a new theme with the words 'Turning now to Haiafi' aroused curiosity. It was not immediately apparent that he was about to embark on the Palestine problem. But this transmogrification did not have quite such a compelling effect as some of his 1946 Peace Conference interpretations in Paris, where, for instance, the Alpine villages of Briga and Tenda were invariably referred to as Brenda and Tiger, which somehow reduced the whole problem to Whipsnade proportions.

Rab was very much aware how unsatisfactory the final result was of a speech put together from the jottings of the different departments. But like most Ministers he was ready, and even eager, to have a draft upon which to work. His habit was to take it to the large conference table at the end of the room and go through it with one of the Private Secretaries, spreading it out like the pieces of a suit and then trying to stitch it together into some sort of shape. It was an amusing and an instructive experience. Making his way one morning through a particularly unco-ordinated collection of platitudes dished up by the Office he turned to me and said: 'I think the dog's dinner begins to sniff badly about here.' Then a little further on: 'Don't you think there's too much of the Lassie touch about this piece?'

Rab liked dog metaphors because he loved dogs. One Saturday morning I was in the office with my dog. Rab telephoned from the country. While we were speaking a messenger came into the Private Office with a red box. This made my dog bark. 'What's that?' Rab asked, showing more interest than he had done in the Yemen situation which we had been discussing. 'I'm sorry,' I said. 'It's my dog.' 'How nice,' he replied. 'Is he with you? How nice. What sort is he?'

One weekday not long afterwards Rab said that he wanted to try to leave the office early that evening so as to be able to get down to his house in Essex for the night. 'Yes, of course,' I said. 'Mrs Butler's down there, isn't she?' 'It's my Dandie Dinmont,' Rab said. 'He's killing. Mollie's got some new covers and I must see what he's done to them.' He caught the 5.20 train.

Anything to do with animal life diverted Rab. Seated with him at that long table trying in desultory fashion to construct a speech from the rag-bag put up by the Office, it seemed to me on one occasion as though the life would go out of both of us. By way of light relief, I drew his attention to the balustrade on the balcony which ran round outside the window of his room and that of the Private Office. I reminded him of the flocks of pigeons which used to gather there, and I told him of the pigeon repellent which we had had to have put down in order to keep them away. 'Oh, why did you do that?' he asked. 'Well, you couldn't see them when you were sitting at your desk because you had your back to the window. But that parapet', I explained, 'used to be one of the pigeons' favourite trysting places in Whitehall.' He looked interested. 'Yes; you may have thought that that look of rapt attention on the face of visitors seated opposite you arose from their interest in what you were saying. But in fact more often than not it was the pigeons they were following.' 'Has that really been happening?' Rab asked, vibrant with delight. But then he suggested half-seriously that we had been spoil-sports to order the repellent. I believe that he really thought that we had been wrong to take the side of humans against the animal kingdom.

Rab was conscious of the expense of time and effort which Ministerial speeches caused for the department. 'I don't want to be like Halifax,' he said one day. 'I remember when I was Under-Secretary along the corridor twenty-five years ago, if Halifax was preparing a speech the rest of the work of the Office came to a standstill – we would all have to make admiring comments upon the text.'

Rab went on to insist that he wanted his speeches to be part of the current work and not to hold everything up. It was to be the same with draft answers to parliamentary questions about which he spoke with no false immodesty: 'I think I have had more experience of parliamentary questions than anyone else in the government. I used to take thirty to forty of them in a day.' Yet he was also very demanding of ideas. The department would say for instance that at that moment there was nothing new to say on disarmament. Rab would urge them to think up something 'constructive', a favourite word of his, but they would explain that anything that could be said at that moment had been said already. It was then that Rab showed his politician's flair. 'Well, I'm not going to say that it's all been said before,' he would explain, 'because that will mean that no one will listen.' He proceeded to list the old arguments in a new series of points. These he said he would put right at the start of his speech. The Press could then lift them without effort instead of working through the whole text. 'I've been making speeches for over thirty years,' he would point out, 'and I know that unless you make things easy for the Press and highlight certain points you just won't be reported.' His scheme worked admirably; the Press gave much prominence to Rab's 'Seven-Point Geneva Plan'. He had, it must be admitted, taken trouble to brief both British and American correspondents beforehand. 'I am giving you the main points of my Geneva speech now. This will save you the fare. I can say all I have to say in fifteen minutes, but I'm told I have to speak for an hour to be respectable.'

Rab took a lot of trouble with his speeches. Yet, in accordance with Evelyn Waugh's dictum that, whereas a writer thinks in words, a politician thinks in sentences, he did not seem very sensitive about the individual words. He was not conspicuously afraid of cliché. 'Working on the speech', as he would call the endless process of going through the Office draft, with Tom Bridges or me beside him, he would pause after reading some passage and say, 'I often think I would have made a good sub-editor of the *Evening Standard*. I think I'll add this.' We would wait to see what contribution he was making, but what it usually amounted to was either writing the arguments hitherto made in a numbered catalogue or inserting some such phrase as 'British policy will continue to be constructive in this field'.

No wonder that when a speech prepared in this way came to be delivered in the House of Commons the effect was rarely electric. 'Rab knows how to keep the temperature down,' his friends would say. Yet when he had to wind up and there was no prepared draft, so that he had to rely on his own curious technique of verbal impressionism, the result was effective. The House was always inclined to see brilliant *double entendre* in anything unclear that he said; and his humour was certainly never far below the surface, a matter of delight, needless to say, to the Private Office. He was winding up on one occasion, making much use of brushwork to conceal any weakness in detail. He was conveying a picture of activity, big sweeps across a wide canvas. He said that he had taken to heart the strong views of the House on Cyprus. He would be transmitting these to the Secretary-General of the United Nations, U Thant. Then he added with a slight chuckle: 'And I know that he, as a good parliamentarian, will understand and give them due attention.' This went down well.

The next day, during a post-mortem on the debate, I said, 'I gather by the way that Burma has no parliament and that U Thant has never been a parliamentarian. He was a schoolmaster, so we were all tickled by the passage in your speech about him.' 'No. Did I say that!' he exclaimed, and his face, till that moment sad and Grocklike, dissolved in laughter.

His reputation for innuendoes had become international, as we discovered during a visit to Copenhagen, where Rab went to deliver a speech which Alec Douglas-Home, during his tenure of office, had committed the Foreign Secretary to giving. Rab began

like this: 'Sir Alec Douglas-Home accepted the invitation to ad-
dress you. I am here in his place. I am honoured to be here. But I
wish it could have been him who was here tonight ...' The Dan-
ish audience laughed for a long time – as they did also later in the
speech when he spoke of Denmark and Britain both being small
countries.

On a visit to the USSR in the summer of 1964 Rab paid a call,
as one academic to another, on the Rector of Moscow University.
A large throng of British journalists was in attendance. He listened, visibly bored, while the Rector, an elderly mathematician,
gave some facts about the number of students, teachers, etc.
Then, invited to put questions, Rab asked: 'Does the university
get any financial support from the state?' Taken aback, the Rector
explained that in a Communist society the university depends
entirely upon state finances.

Afterwards, I joined the British journalists. 'So typical of Rab,'
one of them said. 'Did you see how he led the Rector on with that
dead-pan question. He just wanted to get a reaction, and the Rector fell right into the trap.'

But his reputation for subtlety did not always stand him in
good stead. During a visit to Washington for a CENTO meeting
in May 1965, he delivered a speech which had been prepared entirely by the department. He hardly looked at it beforehand. But
reading it through in bed the previous night he decided that it
was rather long. He therefore deleted two paragraphs about his
attitude to a UN force, which he regarded as irrelevant to
CENTO's immediate proceedings. Unfortunately, the full text
had been given in advance to the Press, which ignored the code of
checking before delivery. The newspapers made much of the

omitted passages; they alleged that they meant that the Foreign Secretary had lost his earlier interest in the UN peace-keeping machinery. As a result the speech attained more publicity in the UK than any Rab was to deliver during his time as Foreign Secretary. He probably spent less time on it than on any other speech, and the passages which attracted all the attention were those he had never delivered. 'I give up trying to understand the British Press,' he said to me in his philosophical, unembittered way.

It is usually extraneous factors, particularly the place and time, which make or mar a speech, not the actual content. One of the most famous examples of this, so far as Foreign Secretaries' speeches are concerned, was the great acclaim given to Samuel Hoare's speech on Collective Security, delivered at Geneva in September 1935. What he said there, he wrote in his autobiography, he 'had already said over and over again, and no one had been particularly excited. Was there ever a better example of the fact that in nine cases out of ten it is the occasion that makes the speech and not the speech the occasion?'[9]

The Press naturally loved Rab's unfailing indiscretions, as did the Office. Young counsellors from the departments, summoned to his room for a discussion on some burning issue, for example Cyprus, were astonished to hear him giving his views on his Cabinet colleagues, on the Conservative Party or on the conduct of Cabinet business. 'What you are forgetting', he said obliquely one day at an Office meeting, 'is that I am a member of the Conservative Party which I have the honour to represent …' Apropos of nothing in particular he soliloquized thus: 'I was chairman of the

---

9 Lord Templewood, *Nine Troubled Years*, p. 170.

Home Affairs Committee for six years and I know how to take a meeting. I like taking a meeting. Mind you, Alec is not bad.' He was often a little patronizing about the Prime Minister, but never disloyal. He would tilt his chair back, apply his empty spectacle case to his nose and speculate on how he could help Home. 'He's a good man, Alec,' he would say time and again speaking out of the side of his face. But there was nothing of an intriguer about Rab – evident from his failures to get to No. 10 – and I never heard him say anything suggesting that he was trying to usurp the Prime Minister's responsibility or to take the limelight from him. Coming into the office the morning Iain Macleod's article had been published, giving his account of the succession crisis in which Home had become Prime Minister, Rab said to me rhetorically, 'I do not think it will help much, do you?' When I replied that he, Rab, had not come badly out of the article, he commented, 'Almost like a fairy story, isn't it?' adding, 'Well, in Cabinet today I propose saying that I think we should all stick close behind Alec.'

The following year, after Rab had left politics, I ran into him in the foyer of the Festival Hall. The news of Home's resignation as leader of the Tory Party had just been announced. Rab, who was hating every moment of the Bolshoi Ballet and looking for someone to be indiscreet to, tacked himself on to my party.

'It's all so sad, isn't it?' he said to me. 'I mean, Mollie says it shows I made a great mistake [i.e. to give up the chance to succeed Home], but you don't think so, do you? I say it's very sad. I mean for Alec.'

As I have said, Rab had a clear idea of what his role was in the Foreign Office as distinct from that of the officials. Discussing the desirability of a conference on Cambodia, he suspected that we might be missing the bus by not having one. 'I knew the Americans didn't want one; and we have been right not to press for one last December [1963], but my political nose begins to itch and to tell me that we should not put it off much longer. After all, that's what you have me here for, isn't it?'

He was a great one for rhetorical questions. Seeing Monsieur Erkin, the Turkish Foreign Minister, about the Cyprus situation, he said: 'You see, we are not in Cyprus for imperial reasons, are we?' He also loved *non sequiturs*. Referring to a Guatemalan, a member of the UN Secretariat who had been sent by U Thant to see him, he commented to his staff, 'He seems quite a decent man, doesn't he? I mean Duncan [Sandys] and I have been quite taken with him, which is why we are so pleased to make progress.'

In the summer of 1964, which we knew to be only a few months from the general election, Rab decided to have his portrait painted in the office. We tried to persuade him to put it off to the summer recess, but he was adamant that it should proceed. 'Other people', he said plaintively one morning to a member of the Private Office, 'spend their time in getting to No. 10, so I don't see why I should not have my picture painted by a first-rate artist.' The artist was Allan Gwynne-Jones. Rab said that Kenneth Clark had recommended him as the best, or he would not have chosen him. Peterhouse College was paying for the picture.

There were over forty hours of sittings, each of them usually from 9 to 1 a.m. One of the Private Secretaries would have to go into the office to give Rab the gist of the telegrams and discuss the work of the day during the sittings when he was staring inscrutably out of the window on to St James's Park. The disclosures were much to the interest of the artist and to the concern of those responsible for security. When the sittings were over for the day, the easel and canvas would remain in the room so that we always felt that we had Rab with us even when in fact he was away at some meeting. Gwynne-Jones quickly achieved an uncanny likeness. 'The trouble will come', he told us Private Secretaries as we foregathered in front of the canvas one morning after Rab had gone out, 'when we get to the mouth and chin. But I am not going to shirk them. They must all go down. And the line here', he pointed to the junction of neck and body, 'is really very beautiful.' We looked carefully.

'You see what I am trying to do,' Gwynne-Jones said to us one morning, covering the face with a cloth, leaving visible only the neck and shoulders. 'Even without the face altogether you would recognize who it was … but I am trying to show the essential niceness of the man. The other day I had the picture down in the country and some friends came in to see it. "What a nice man," they exclaimed.'

There was nothing reserved about Rab, and he liked to tell you what he thought about everyone and how he got on with them. Beaverbrook and Randolph Churchill, he disclosed, were his only enemies. Referring to Harold Macmillan's 'They have never had it so good' statement of a few years back, he volunteered: 'You know I used to tell Harold that he was like Guizot who said "Enrichissez-vous", but as Guizot did not last long, Harold didn't like it much.' Chuckle, chuckle.

His confidences, his indiscretions, his humour, his good temper, his imperturbability and the readiness with which he bared his soul – these qualities made Rab a very great pleasure to work for. He was also full of worldly wisdom, which, without being at all didactic, he was always ready to impart. I think I learned more in one year from Rab about political life than I did from anyone else I have served for however long. The Office, in suggesting the wording of an announcement about Rab's travel plans, were apt to want to say: Mr R. A. Butler will be visiting such and such a country on a fact-finding mission (or to familiarize himself with the latest situation there). Rab would delete this, saying that the British Foreign Secretary did not travel abroad to learn but to give advice and impart information about British policy.

One of the beneficial side-effects of working for Rab was that I saw quite a bit of Alec Douglas-Home as Prime Minister. In July 1964 Rab had been persuaded to invite the Turkish Prime Minister, Inönü, to a small dinner party one Sunday evening at No. 1 Carlton Gardens. The party consisted of Inönü and four Turks on one side; on the other side, Rab, the Prime Minister, Carrington, Sandys, Caccia, Derek Dodson[10] and myself. It had been agreed that the Prime Minister would arrive half an hour in advance so as to compare notes before the meeting. The briefing was to be short – how Home liked it. Butler said: 'I don't know how we are going to get through the evening, whether we are going to talk about procedure or really get down to the future of Cyprus.' The Prime Minister said: 'The important thing is how are we going to bring the dinner party to a close.'

We then descended to the official apartment below to greet the guests.

---

10 Derek Dodson, diplomat, at that time Head of Central Department, Foreign Office; later Ambassador to Hungary, Brazil and Turkey.

Inönü held the fate of Turkey in his hands and had been alone responsible, so we were told, for the fact that the Turks had not so far invaded Cyprus. A small, deaf, very old man, the outstanding feature of his personality was his presumption that everyone wished to listen and to heed him, as indeed his compatriots had done for half a century. Through the Ambassador, acting as interpreter, he delivered a monologue during dinner, paying little attention to his audience, but a great deal to his food. Informed beforehand that he was a diabetic, Government Hospitality had proudly laid on special food. We were astonished to find that he did not scruple to wave their selection aside and ask for other dishes, now caviare, now cheeses, as if he was in a restaurant. When, after consuming these, he dismissed the lavish cornucopia of fruit offered him and asked for more cheese, we on our side had difficulty in restraining our laughter. The Prime Minister, accustomed though he was to eccentrics, had the giggles from early on in the evening because, on arrival, the Turkish Ambassador, acting he said on the orders of Inönü , had insisted on altering the whole table plan so as to permit the Turkish party to sit side by side. We had protested that this would make conversation difficult and that it would mean that the Prime Minister and Inönü would be very far apart. But they were adamant. So there we were, seated like teams either side of the table, with Inönü, looking like Mickey Mouse, asking continually for cheese, and holding forth in Turkish, too deaf to hear the Prime Minister's polite attempts to get a word in. The officials on our side were delighted and congratulated themselves on belonging to a profession that could mount so serious an occasion.

I cannot exaggerate the opportunity and pleasure the Private

Secretary can secure from casual conversation with his master, in cars, airports or planes, a chance that is not afforded to anyone else.

Rab often reminisced: 'You know, I never said, "Eden is the best Prime Minister we have." What happened was this. At the beginning of 1956 Eden was being attacked in the Press. I was going off from London airport on some mission and I was asked whether I thought Eden was the best Prime Minister we had. I said, "Yes." That's all there is to it.' This rebuttal did not strike me as very convincing, but I listened sympathetically as Rab moved on to Suez: 'Of course the Party held that against me but I was not disloyal to Eden. I was critical because I thought it mismanaged. Being the son of a civil servant I also thought it wrong to treat officials as Eden did over Suez. I didn't like the collusion either. *I should have resigned, shouldn't I?*'

Rab's last weeks as Foreign Secretary were sad. Bored stiff with the election, he would come frequently to the office. I sought his comment on the latest opinion poll that, contrary to earlier predictions, now favoured the Tories' chances. The only response I got was his favourite, somewhat equivocal, 'Yes' and a look of profound gloom. Reading the Prime Minister's speeches appeared to have the same effect upon him as had the reading of Palmerston's dispatches upon Queen Victoria.

His innate indiscretion suddenly got the better of him. A matter of days before the poll, the *Daily Express* published what purported to be an interview with him in the course of a train journey to Warrington where he was speaking. He allegedly said that the Tories were going to lose the election, that the Prime Minister had been wrong in saying that there was a draft non-dissemination treaty, that Hogg had been misguided in providing the occasion that had revived the Profumo affair, and that Alec Douglas-Home found Ted Heath 'a bore'.

The telephone shrieked throughout the morning. The Conservative Central Office were furious to have Tory confidence undermined at this crucial moment. Rab telephoned Heath's office asking his Private Secretary to assure the Minister that the 'bore' story was a travesty. With characteristic generosity the Prime Minister telephoned Rab a few days after the *Daily Express* story. 'Hello, Rab,' he said cheerfully. 'Sorry I was not able to reach you before; I wanted to tell you not to bother about that stupid *Express* story, couldn't have mattered less.'

Whatever the consequences of this particular episode, there is no doubt that Rab's career as a whole had benefited enormously from his unfailing indiscretion. He was inclined to reveal even more to the Press than he did to officials, though he was scarcely reticent with us. I must say I got the impression that Rab had decided well before the poll that the Conservatives were going to lose. It was one of the reasons that made him so gloomy, and even sentimental about the Office.

When, after Labour had won the election, the time came for Rab to make way for Gordon Walker, his departure had a look of Greek tragedy about it. Realizing that after some forty years in public life he would never hold office again, he clearly did not intend to skimp his farewell performance. He told us how happy our prospects were compared with his. He would miss it all very much. It would never be the same again. Renouncing the use of an official car and stepping out from the side door of the Foreign Office into the Horse Guards, his withered arm at his side, he set off across the park glancing up at the sky as if he saw in its new-found limitlessness something as full of foreboding as did Oscar Wilde's condemned murderer in looking up at the little tent of blue. He was a free man, yet after all those years he dreaded being without the bonds of office.

On the day Winston Churchill retired from office in 1955 Rab sent him the following lines of St Teresa of Avila:

> Let nothing disturb thee,
> Let nothing affright thee,
> All passeth away,
> God alone will stay,
> Patience obtaineth all things.

Was he muttering these words to himself as he left office for the last time?

7

CHANGE OF REGIME

My most vivid recollection of the change of regime after the 1964 general election was the sense of euphoria suddenly let loose. Labour Ministers were in a high state of excitement at being in office after so long in the wilderness. A member of the Cabinet told me that at the first meeting of Ministers in October 1964 there was one thing that they all had in common, happiness at being in the Promised Land at last. The poll may have been a close-run thing, and government would be bound to prove difficult with so slender a majority in the Commons, but it was enough for the moment that Labour were occupying the seats of power and that the Tories were nowhere.

It was exciting to feel the power of the Civil Service behind, instead of against, them. But they were a little in awe of this very power. The main contrast between this hand-over and that of 1945 was that Labour had been out of office for thirteen years, whereas Bevin and many others in Attlee's administration had been senior members of a coalition government that had only ceased to govern a few months earlier. On this occasion, suspicion

Gordon Walker and the author.

was added to inexperience. Many Ministers feared that the officials would withhold information from them and try to run things their own way and against that of their political masters. This partly explains, I think, the decision taken almost immediately after the election to levy an import surcharge on manufactures without any prior consultation with EFTA[1] countries, as required by the Stockholm Agreement; officials warned them of the likely repercussions, but they might have done so more cate-

---

1 The European Free Trade Association, established in 1959 by seven states which were not prepared to accept the political implications of the European Economic Community.

gorically had they not been afraid of exciting the charge of being anti-Labour. It took time for trust to be established.

Looking back to those two decades after the war, it is interesting to question how much difference there was in practice between Conservative and Labour politicians in the actual conduct of foreign policy.

True, Attlee pulled out of India more quickly than Churchill would probably have done. But Labour could scarcely have left Africa sooner than Macmillan did, in fulfilment of his 'winds of change' forecast. However much lip-service Tory leaders paid in opposition, 1945–51, to the importance of closer UK relations with a more unified Europe, they did little about it when they were in power during the next thirteen years, until their belated and unsuccessful attempt to get into the European Economic Community at the very end of their tenure; while Labour leaders, though inherently suspicious of European involvement and sceptical in opposition of the value of UK entry to the EEC, became marketeers in government, some admittedly keener than others. Towards the Commonwealth, Labour politicians showed enthusiasm before 1964, and they were scathing about the lack of proper interest shown by the Conservative Government; but they had not been in office long before they accepted the realities of the Commonwealth connection.

The pre-1964 Labour platform included the promise to get rid of the UK's independent nuclear deterrent, a pledge which Alec Douglas-Home criticized strongly in the electoral campaign. But somehow they managed to shove the commitment under the rug as soon as they were in power; the deterrent was allowed to survive.

However, there were important differences. Though sceptical of too close a link with Europe, the Labour leaders of 1964 believed in the solidarity of Social Democratic governments. When they ran into stiff opposition from the EFTA countries for their suddenly imposed import surcharge, Gordon Walker said, 'I'm a great believer in appealing to Sweden and Denmark and the other Socialist governments as like-minded, and therefore friendly powers.' Despite the hard historical evidence against expecting benefits to flow across national frontiers for reasons of political affinity (e.g. one of the first and most striking examples in the modern age was when the French Monarchy supported the American revolutionaries), Labour leaders are most reluctant to renounce such hopes.

Though the British public, allergic to Nasser and drawn to Eden, may well have supported the Suez affair once it was launched, it is difficult to believe that a Labour Government would ever have embarked upon it. Not only would they have been instinctively less inclined to initiate the use of force in the absence of international support, but, leaving expediency out of account, they would surely have felt certain moral inhibitions. Labour has after all inherited the Gladstonian aura that there is something of a moral crusade in politics, foreign as well as domestic.

Linked with this was a vestigial and half-formulated belief, amongst many Labour old-timers, in the desirable and, indeed, inevitable disappearance of sovereign states, in some brotherhood of man without class or frontiers. These two forces had contributed to an almost atavistic dislike in Labour circles of 'power politics', or 'spheres of influence', let alone of any trigger-happy talk about resort to war. They had helped to give Labour foreign policy its own style and language and they had much to do with the Party's almost messianic faith in the United Nations.

In opposition they had been critical of the lack of fervour shown by the Conservative Government towards the UN: they disliked the attitude Alec Douglas-Home adopted at the UN Assembly in the autumn of 1961, and, even more, his speech at Berwick upon Tweed in December of that year when he deplored the double standard which prevailed in the Assembly – a speech, incidentally, which had done more than anything, in R. A. Butler's view, to seal the love match between Home and the Tory Party. Anyway, to mark their different approach, the Labour Government, on assuming office in 1964, immediately appointed a Minister in the Government to be their permanent representative to the UN. As events were soon to show, they found that this made little difference in practice and that Afro-Asian opinion was not to be placated by gestures. Before long George Brown, as Foreign Secretary, was making the same old complaint about the same old double standard (UN Assembly, September 1967) as Home had done.

Mention has been made earlier of Bevin's conviction, expressed soon after becoming Foreign Secretary, that the Labour Government were capturing the moral leadership of the world. Twenty years later, Ministers in the second post-war Labour Government quickly convinced themselves that they were leading the same successful crusade. As ready as the Tories to act in defence of British interests anywhere, they wanted nevertheless to make it clear to the world that they were acting defensively and in support of international order; and their language had to strike an almost evangelical note. Michael Stewart had not been long in Palmerston's seat before he was talking in a most un-Palmerstonian way of his belief in international law, by which he meant international order and the rule of law. He hoped that one day there would be a code of conduct between nations, such as already existed between individuals within a state, and that it would be as enforceable as a country's internal law. He thought that Britain should be prepared to make sacrifices as a nation in the interests of helping to bring about the rule of international society. In the UN for instance we must be ready to waive the veto and accept the verdict of the organization, even if this meant giving up some immediate national advantage. We must also avoid doing things which, though we might get away with them, were fundamentally in conflict with the rule of law in international life.

At one moment the department were urging Stewart to agree to some proposal in the Middle East that might have led to the use of force, but no, the Secretary of State said that the use of force was contrary to the rule of law; other means must be found of achieving the desired end. 'You see, it's like with the chimney boys. It was only when a law was passed in the last century making it illegal to use children to go up chimneys, that alternative methods were devised for cleaning them. So, I believe, in international affairs ...'

As I listened, it occurred to me that you would not have heard a Conservative Foreign Secretary invoking the lesson of chimney boys in this way. Labour impulses were different in the foreign, as in the domestic, field, however similar the general direction of policy. Many Labour leaders coming to office in 1964 were as imbued as their predecessors had been twenty years before with the need for Britain to set an example to the world. Michael Stewart used to tell his staff at Office meetings that HMG had a duty to behave in a certain honourable way in international affairs, and that if they did so, other countries would be disposed to follow. Thus he suggested in the spring of 1965 that we should make an unconditional offer of money (eight million dollars) to the UN to bail it out of its economic predicament. He was confident that this would serve as an example, and that other countries would soon follow suit and cough up money. This was the sort of language he had used in a public speech to the Press Club in Washington shortly before. Speaking of the reported use by the US forces of poison gas in Vietnam, he counselled the administration to follow the precept of the Declaration of Independence and have 'a proper respect for the opinion of mankind'. But Michael Stewart was not alone in this moral approach to foreign affairs which prevailed at any rate in the opening months of the Labour administration. Barbara Castle, in charge of overseas aid, was insistent that financial help should be given to those countries most in need and that, in deciding which to choose, absolutely no regard should be had to possible later benefits to HMG.

Lord Chalfont, whom Harold Wilson had appointed Minister of State at the FCO in charge of disarmament, put forward the idea that Britain should renounce her nuclear weapons in order to set an example to other countries and induce them to accept a non-dissemination agreement. The proposal was discussed at a large Office meeting held by the Secretary of State. Everybody realized the importance of devising some means by which India could be given security and dissuaded from producing an atomic bomb. But no one could see how India was going to be made to feel safer in the face of the Chinese, or be induced to renounce the production of atomic weapons to deter the Chinese, merely because we had set the example of scrapping our bomb.

Not many days after this, I had a word with Con O'Neill about Labour's devotion to rule by example in foreign policy. 'Yes,' he said, fired by the idea, 'and the weaker we are, the more we seem to expect people to follow our example. It's almost as though it were a substitute for power. Yet what a nonsense it is. Can you think of a single example in history of one country following a good example set by another? There are plenty of instances of countries following bad examples.'

As events were to show, the rest of the world did not seem inclined in the next few years to imitate what we regarded as our exemplary international behaviour; and before long complaints began to be heard in Press and Parliament that Britain was being pushed around. The Algerian government, for instance, detained in prison for three months in 1967 two British civil pilots whose plane, carrying Tshombe, had been hijacked. That this was unpardonable and unprecedented international behaviour did not seem to worry the Algerian government in the slightest. HMG had no appropriate means of counter-pressure on Algeria, a country dedicated to an anti-British policy as a result of Rhodesia and the Six Days War. Likewise, over Gibraltar, mere pleas for a 'reasonable' attitude on the part of Spain were ineffective in the absence of counter-measures. The example of sweet reasonableness on our part was regarded by the Spaniards as derisory humbug so long as we were not prepared to give them what they wanted. To the Spanish government, as to others, the precedents of Ireland and Palestine may have helped to guide them in choosing the best tactics to adopt in dealing with the British. From the way Madrid behaved over Gibraltar after Labour's return to power in October 1964, it seemed as though they looked at these earlier historical parallels and came to the conclusion that the best way to get the British to yield was to kick them in the teeth.

Yet Michael Stewart did not believe that achievement of a quiet life should be the be-all and end-all of British policy. We had to fulfil our obligations, e.g. to stand up for the rights of the inhabitants of some tiny territory, even though this meant conflict with a much more important country which was claiming sovereignty over it, as in Gibraltar or the Falkland Islands. Principles to him were two-way, to be respected by others as well as ourselves, which did not make for an easy time, given our weakness. Britain was in clear retreat as a world power, at a greater rate immediately after 1964 than in any previous era in her history. The abandonment of India just after the war did, of course, dramatically mark our changed role in the world; and Suez was certainly both pointer and stimulant to decline. But the consequences in terms of world power and influence were masked for a long time, with the result, among others, that we had failed to join the EEC in its formative phase when we could have influenced its design. There was no concealing our weakness by the mid-sixties, and a high moral tone proved to be all the more difficult to sustain in the face of dwindling material means.

When, in the days of the first Labour Government after the war, Bevin had taken the initiative and thrown out the ideas which eventually took shape in the European Recovery Programme and NATO, other countries in Europe responded, because they were weak and Britain was relatively strong; and the

US listened because we had influence. At the time of the Korean War Truman listened to Attlee, but there was little sign that Johnson was interested in Wilson's advice over Vietnam. By the sixties we had lost our former position not only in the Middle and Far East, but in Europe. De Gaulle could keep us out of the EEC, and no other country in Western Europe dared to say boo to him; we were not worth a detour for any of the five. This was so whether there was a Conservative or a Labour Government in London. It made little difference in practice who was in power, and once Labour politicians had surmounted their initial inhibitions about Europe, they urged British entry as the Tories had done. But as always their language was different and Harold Wilson stressed the technological contribution we could make to Europe.

Living close in the Private Office to the day-to-day decisions of successive Conservative and Labour Governments in the forties and sixties, it was impossible not to sense the many underlying similarities of policy in defence of national interests; but also the considerable contrast between the leaders of the two Parties in the style and flexibility with which they spoke and acted. It was easier in any case for Attlee and Bevin than for their successors twenty years later, because of Britain's comparatively greater military and economic strength in relation to other countries; and, looking back, it is easy to see how the absence of power in the sixties undermined Labour's approach to foreign policy.

After the October 1964 general election, Gordon Walker was beginning to show his paces by the time he was rejected three months later by the Leyton electorate. His wife had endeared herself to us in the Private Office by her understanding of the personal problems posed by the change of government. Mrs Gordon

Walker described her first visit to Dorneywood, the country house made available for the use of the Foreign Secretary thanks to the generosity of its owner, Lord Courtauld-Thomson, who had given it to the nation with a large endowment. The housekeeper had spoken incessantly of the Homes whom she adored. She said that all the curtains had been cleaned: 'Such a pity the Homes were not able to enjoy them looking so pretty.' Mrs Gordon Walker said she felt like the second wife in *Rebecca*. According to Michael Stewart, the housekeeper, who had been in the employ of Lord Courtauld-Thomson, always referred to Lord Home as 'The Lord', thus distinguishing him from Lord Courtauld-Thomson whom she described as 'Our Lord'.[2]

I only spent one night at Dorneywood. It is beautifully furnished and very comfortable. I was there in December 1964, when Gordon Walker entertained his German opposite number, Schroeder. He was accompanied by his Private Secretary, Simon. There was just the dinner, the night, breakfast, and then off. It was all quite easy, and within strict limits useful. I could see what a boon the house could be to the Foreign Secretary; and how valuable in certain circumstances it could be for entertaining distinguished foreign visitors informally.

My own memory is dominated by the figure of the old housekeeper whom I have just mentioned. She was very much in evidence that night when the German Foreign Minister was there. He had to leave early the following morning by air from London airport. I undertook to accompany him there. The housekeeper promised to call us all in sufficient time. For some reason she

2 Michael Stewart, *Life and Labour*, p. 183.

omitted to call me, so that I was still asleep a few minutes before Schroeder was due to leave the house. The Gordon Walkers sent her up to me hurriedly. She shook me violently:

'Naughty thing,' she said, 'you naughty thing, going to sleep again, after I woke you up.'

Gordon Walker favoured a seminar approach for getting to grips with a problem and deciding upon policy. This also enabled him to sum people up as suitable or not for the vacancies in the higher reaches of the Office. So it was that, soon after he became Foreign Minister, he called a meeting of British ambassadors from NATO countries. The agenda was to discuss the Government's tentative ideas for a new nuclear defence force, incorporating the multilateral force (MLF), and to consider what General de Gaulle was likely to do in his next campaigning season against us and how we might respond. The meeting proved to be reminiscent of the country house test that had to be taken by all those entering the Foreign Office after World War II. The background presented now to the ambassadors was uncannily like the scenario of the exercise when I had been a candidate nearly twenty years before: an island in severe economic difficulties, whose interests were persistently threatened by an unpredictable strong man in a neighbouring country. The ambassadors, seated like students round a table, with carefully prepared notes, were competing, though ostensibly co-operating, to meet the needs of the new Foreign Secretary.

It is difficult to exaggerate how overpowering for Western Europe in general and for the UK in particular was the looming presence at this time of de Gaulle. Paul-Henri Spaak, the eminent Belgian Foreign Minister, came over to London for a day's visit to tell us about it. He had recently seen the General, whom he described as '*très pessimiste et très détaché*'. Not having been responsible for the creation of either NATO or the Common Market, the General was not really interested in either of them. He had, according to Spaak, a clear idea of what it means to be a good European: from the moment Britain had signed the Nassau Agreement with the Americans they had ceased to be Europeans and had been ostracized by the General, as in his exclusion *coup* of 14 January 1963; from the time the Germans had become involved with the Americans in the MLF in a way the General did not like because it might well have produced a surface US/European fleet, he had dismissed them as bad Europeans and turned his invective upon them; the Belgians, once they had relied upon the help of the USA over the recent Stanleyville Operation, had likewise been cold-shouldered by de Gaulle. As the General saw it, Spaak explained unemotionally and pellucidly, wise and massive as he sat opposite the vast eighteenth-century portraits in the Ambassadors' Waiting Room where we were meeting, it was not possible to be a good European if you also had close relations with the USA. European countries must choose between Europe and America. It was de Gaulle's destiny, he believed, to sever European dependence on the USA.

At the beginning of 1965 I took stock of what, over the previous few months, had seemed to be the outstanding features of the international scene as viewed from the British standpoint. It did not appear to have been the change of government in London (despite the new drum-beat to the god of technology) nor the substitution of Brezhnev for Khrushchev in Moscow, nor the crisis in the Congo, not Vietnam, not the uncertainties over

Sukarno's health, not the revolution in the Sudan, not even the appalling weakness of sterling – important though all these events had been. No, it was the dominance of de Gaulle. He had only to whisper over grain prices for Germany to shiver, or over the MLF for the Atlantic to recede. The Paris Embassy continued to insist that he meant to bust up the Common Market and NATO, but it did not really look as though he needed to do anything to bring this about. He could make them dance to his tune by the merest threat. Nor did anyone else in the western world look like countering him. Washington, involved in Vietnam, seemed to be playing a very quiet role towards Europe. The UK at that moment did not have the influence to affect events. West Germany was awaiting elections. As for Moscow, it seemed wrapped in night following Khrushchev's fall.

During the first weeks of 1965, the time of the Private Office was spent in keeping in touch with the Foreign Secretary, campaigning in his constituency at Leyton. He had established some sort of headquarters in a cold, gloomy room, which normally served as the green room for theatricals in the Town Hall, heated by a small electric log-fire. I suspect that our daily arrival with boxes gave more warmth to the Secretary of State than the heating system, because we brought news from a world where he counted, whereas in Leyton nobody seemed to care for him at all. Many of those who normally would have supported Labour did not like the way their sitting Member had been removed in order to provide a seat for someone who had lost his but was now Foreign Secretary. On the subject of Labour's unpopularity many in the constituency confided uninhibitedly in us, so we were not altogether surprised by the result of the poll in which Gordon

Walker was defeated. We were very much aware of what a personal tragedy it was for him; but we also realized that in some way it was a vindication of the democratic process. Less objectively we knew the consequences for us of having to initiate a new Foreign Secretary into the ways of the Office, the third in fifteen months.

8

AN UNSUNG
FOREIGN SECRETARY

After Michael Stewart, chosen to succeed Gordon Walker, had run the gauntlet of the Press outside the building and entered his grand new office for the first time, he said that he could not think why they had wanted to take so many photographs of him. 'One correspondent', he said, 'didn't seem to know much about politicians because he asked me if I was pleased to be Foreign Secretary. I said that I didn't know anybody in politics who would not like to be Foreign Secretary.' Certainly, it is a glittering prospect: you become a world figure overnight; the circumstances of life – the accommodation at home, the luxurious travel and the outward respect of foreign governments – are flattering; the problems are never dull. But there is more sheer drudgery than many suspect; and though fame comes easily, success is rare.[1]

---

1 'Search the world over, hunt history from beginning to end, and you will conclude as the result of your labours that the great Foreign Minister is almost the rarest bird that flies ... Since Castlereagh and Vienna, it seems to me that we have had one, or possibly two, who can be placed in this class – Palmerston and Salisbury.' F. S. Oliver, *The Endless Adventure*, Vol. III, p. 204.

Michael Stewart with Gromyko.

Not that he was taking over at an easy moment. The Government only had a minuscule majority in the House of Commons and Ministerial spirits were low as was Britain's standing abroad. Our ambassadors from the EFTA countries were called back for a pep talk. Michael Stewart took the chair, but it was George Brown, Secretary of State for Economic Affairs, who harangued them. I sat behind George Brown and was able to perceive the astonishment on the faces of the ambassadors as he put them straight. Of course we were unpopular. We had had to do a lot of very unpopular things during the first three months of office after the mess the Tories had left the country in ... but no government in the world had done in years what Labour had done in months to try to modernize the economy of the country. No other government could have been able to avoid the measures

Labour had had to take, i.e. the 15 per cent import surcharge, to deal with the adverse balance of trade. 'You ambassadors', he declaimed, 'should make sure that foreign governments are aware, because I get the impression they simply do not understand what we are doing. I also think they should be told to help us more.'

One of the ambassadors said that the German figures of time lost in strikes gave a much better record for them than did the UK figures for the UK, contrary to what the Secretary of State had just said. George Brown dismissed this as an assertion based on bad statistics. He was not assuaged by the other remarks or questions of the assembled ambassadors. On the way out of the meeting someone from the Office thanked him for coming and said that they hoped he had found it useful. To which George Brown delivered a stricture on ambassadors: 'They are meant to carry out policy which we Ministers lay down, not initiate it as they seem to think they should do.'

In the Private Office we soon realized that Michael Stewart's quietness and unobtrusiveness did not reflect any lack of confidence in his own abilities. He believed that reason rather than ranting should be brought to bear on public issues. He was subjected to prolonged questioning at a Press Conference one day, and a member of the Private Office said to him in the car afterwards that it was noticeable how much he really tried to answer the queries, whereas some politicians seemed to think that the main aim was to say as little as possible in quite a lot of words. 'Yes,' Michael Stewart replied, and it appeared as though that might be the customarily laconic end of it. But he went on: 'I suppose it's having been a schoolmaster for ten years. One cannot eradicate the habit of answering problems put to one.'

This quality of patient exposition was displayed dramatically at the Oxford Teach-In on Vietnam which, thanks to television, established his reputation throughout the country overnight as a formidable debater. Teach-Ins were enjoying a great vogue in the USA at that time; they were just spreading to Britain, and the Vietnam war was the favourite theme for day-long discussion.

When the Office first heard of the invitation to the Foreign Secretary to attend the Oxford Teach-In many doubts were raised: it would be Communist-controlled; the Secretary of State would not get a hearing; he would be humiliated; and he was too big a gun. Michael Stewart listened patiently, said little but concluded: 'I think I can do it. I will go.' He explained to me that it was no good preaching democracy if you shunned such occasions. I telephoned David Caute, a Fellow of All Souls, who was organizing the Teach-In, to say that the Secretary of State agreed to attend. He asked if the Foreign Secretary would waive the rules about advance notice for Soviet officials wishing to travel outside London so as to permit the *Izvestiya* correspondent to come and speak, as he was anxious to do. He spoke to me of the value of democracy and the importance of free speech. Did I not agree that it was one of the things that differentiated our society from that of the Soviet Union? I promised to consult the Foreign Secretary and to ring him back. But I said that the *Izvestiya* man must apply or we could do nothing to help him. I consulted Michael Stewart who agreed to make an exception to the rules. I then rang back Caute who was delighted. He said he would urge the Russian to apply immediately. However, no application was made, so presumably the Russian had cold feet which he had hoped to hide behind our hard, undemocratic rules.

The Secretary of State wanted to be sure that the US case on Vietnam was put by an American. He did not wish to get into the position of being their advocate. His task would be to explain British policy. There was much telephoning between London and Washington. David Bruce[2] was told that he must not speak. It was decided eventually that Cabot Lodge[3] should fly over specially for the occasion – presumably to demonstrate the bi-partisan nature of the US commitment.

The Teach-In was due to take place on a Wednesday. We had only heard about it for the first time on the previous Monday morning. Wherever I went during the intervening two days I found astonishment at the Secretary of State's decision to attend: it would be an extreme left-wing audience; he would be routed. These were the views I received in and out of the Office; and when, after driving from London in the rain, we eventually arrived in the hall of the Oxford Union at 8.30 on the Wednesday evening I did, I must admit, have a moment of doubt whether these sceptics might not have been right. It looked very much as though we had walked into a trap. The house was packed, the atmosphere electric, with the current very obviously running against the Government. James Fawcett,[4] an old friend, who had spoken earlier in the day and who was sitting near the Chair, made a prayerful gesture in my direction and whispered that we were in for a rough time. Peregrine Worsthorne said the same and added that Cabot Lodge had not done well. The gallery, like the

2 David Bruce, US diplomat. Served as US Ambassador to London 1961–9.
3 Cabot Lodge, American politician. Ambassador to Republic of Vietnam 1963–4 and 1965–7.
4 James Fawcett, lawyer. Fellow of All Souls College 1938 and 1960–9.

body of the hall, was overflowing, everyone leaning forward expectantly as in a crowded bullring before the release of the noblest bull; and over the whole scene the TV cameras hovered, ready for blood.

Michael Stewart launched straight in, uncompromising in substance, unprovocative in manner. He was glad to be there. He believed that these Teach-Ins were useful. He looked forward to the day when they were held in Peking, Hanoi and Moscow, as well as in the USA and UK. He explained, as a matter of hard fact, that the Communists were responsible for invading South Vietnam from the North, and that the US Government had only recently begun to retaliate. At this a low murmur of dissent rolled through the hall, but there was no complete interruption. Unperturbed, he went on to say that the USA were ready for talks without conditions, the Communists not. Finally he outlined a possible basis for a settlement, similar to that given to the House of Commons a few weeks before which had received little publicity (in striking contrast, as Michael Stewart pointed out to me afterwards, to the immense publicity it was to get from the Teach-In).

Stewart spoke with scarcely a note. He had memorized large passages, so that the Foreign Office News Department could put them out in advance. He never hesitated. He sat down to enormous applause. It had been a *tour de force*, as the TV commentator described it.

He was then subjected to forty-five minutes of searching, hostile questions. One person asked him how he could favour negotiations when the USA were bombing North Vietnam. Michael Stewart repeated the question, rephrasing it slightly to make it even starker. There were cheers and jeers from the hall as if to say, 'Ha, ha, the Foreign Secretary won't be able to get out of that one.' Many parts of the audience were seething with frustration at the effectiveness of his speech. 'Well,' he said very calmly, rather like a schoolmaster with an unruly class which he knows he can dominate with his tongue rather than his lungs, 'that is not the position the Communist Party of Great Britain took up in 1940 when the Nazis were bombing London and they were all for the British Government negotiating with Germany'. This thrust hurt. I asked the Foreign Secretary afterwards how the parallel had sprung so quickly to mind. He replied, 'I owe that to Pavitt [his Parliamentary Private Secretary] with whom I was discussing the subject in the House the other day.'

There was a difficult moment, I thought, when one questioner accused the Foreign Secretary of misrepresenting the views of the North Vietnam Government: they had not insisted, as Michael Stewart maintained, on the withdrawal of US troops and the representation of the Vietcong, before agreeing to talks; moreover, the questioner had in his hand Hanoi's declaration of April in which neither of these points was raised. He held a piece of paper triumphantly above his head as if to prove his argument. Undeterred, Michael Stewart said, 'But the declaration does contain these two conditions I mentioned; you see.'

The questioner, who by now had some of the audience hysterically behind him, raised the paper even higher and shook his head emphatically, while the hall became a pandemonium.

'Read it, then,' the Secretary of State said very quietly, as soon as the shrieking had subsided. His face bore a seraphic expression of patience: the class could not be expected to advance faster than the pace of its slowest pupil; there was no need to hurry or be angry. The important thing was to teach and persuade.

The questioner began to read; and to my immense relief both of the conditions mentioned by the Secretary of State duly appeared. Again I asked him later in the quiet of his office how he had been so sure that he had remembered this April text from Hanoi so precisely.

'Well,' he said in his most matter-of-fact way, 'that I owe to Warbey because he was always inflicting it on me in the House.'[5]

Somebody else at the Teach-In asked: 'What does the Foreign Secretary say to the fact that the USA have embarked on wholesale aggression against a defenceless country without any justification whatever?'

There was a left-wing roar of triumph, as unmistakable as any hunting-horn. The pack had at last found what they had been looking for, the weakest point in the Foreign Secretary's armour. He was caught at last.

He smiled even more benignly. He swallowed. He put his head a little on one side. He answered: 'Well, I would say that that was a sweeping assertion without any supporting evidence.'

I think it was his distinctive combination of great firmness with extreme quickness which made his whole performance that evening so effective. But it was also his fluency. He did not race. He just went remorselessly on at dictation speed giving no opening for interruptions.

He also understood his audience. This was where Cabot Lodge

---

5 William Warbey, language tutor and interpreter, MP 1945–50, 1953–5 and 1955–66.

failed. He clearly had no idea what a recalcitrant, disrespectful crowd of left-wing undergraduates could be like. We met him for a drink afterwards and he did not conceal his dismay. Generously he congratulated Michael Stewart on his success. He clearly did not at all like the look of modern Oxford undergraduates with their long hair and untidy clothes. Nor did he like their attitude. They had laughed when he had spoken about Churchill. 'They didn't even', he protested indignantly, 'show any admiration for fundamental human virtues like courage.' He then muttered something about the contrast between these youths and the soldiers he had known when he was fighting alongside the British in the last war. I feared it was another case of the Oxford Union being taken at face value by foreigners, as had happened over the King and Country motion in the thirties; for there was no doubt that Cabot Lodge returned to the States the next day with a very poor opinion of the young generation of Britons.

For Michael Stewart the Teach-In evening was a high point in his first spell as Foreign Secretary: he managed to reach and impress the general public. He returned to London like a hero. Yet, as he would have been the first to admit, he had said nothing new: he had merely exploited the occasion to his own advantage with the odds looking stacked against him. Nor did the euphoria endure. Vietnam was to prove a continuing vexation throughout his time as Foreign Secretary. 'The fate of that country', he has written, 'was to prove the most difficult and the most agonizing of all the problems I had to face.'[6]

Michael Stewart was an exceptional debater. He came alive on

---

6 Stewart, *Life and Labour*, p. 151.

his feet. He was able to bring forward from the recesses of his mind some long-stored piece of information. This quality was demonstrated to dramatic effect in a speech he made to a large gathering of political journalists in the House of Commons. He was introduced by the chairman as the forty-seventh in a long line of British Foreign Secretaries which had begun with Charles James Fox. A quotation was read out about Fox's clarity of exposition, and this description was said, with much assenting applause, to be very appropriate to Stewart's public statements. Stewart began very meticulously in reply by expressing his gratitude to the chairman and to the audience. 'I had never imagined myself, he went on, 'as a second Charles James Fox, I must admit.' There was a titter round the room at the sheer incongruity of the idea. 'I have to say too that in one respect I hope I will not emulate him. At one time Fox, despite all his great gifts, had become too much for the government of the day. The Prime Minister decided he must get rid of him. He therefore sent him a note which read, "I enclose a list of the new administration I have formed. I do not see your name among them."'

Michael Stewart then told a couple more political stories, one about Wilkes, the other about a US Senator, before getting on to the serious business of his speech, which was about Europe. The speech as a whole was well received. The clarity of exposition was admired; but what impressed these hard-headed correspondents most was Stewart's ability to draw at will upon his well-stocked memory. For, as the chairman said in thanking him, he had given the Foreign Secretary no warning that he was going to mention Fox.

On a very different occasion – it was aboard *Britannia* where we were sitting around before lunch making desultory conversation about the qualities required for success or failure in public life – Michael Stewart suddenly said: 'I remember a *bon mot* of Ronnie Knox's. He was referring to the traditional English preference for brawn and character over brains. Another way of putting it, Knox suggested, was that the English did not mind bats in the belfry provided they were straight bats.'

He had a habit of dipping into his memory as if it was a way of releasing inner pressure before some great occasion, say a speech to some conference, or upon getting into his car after a difficult bout of parliamentary questions. He would say, for instance, 'It reminds me of a passage in Hardy where he says: …' Hardy, incidentally, was a great literary favourite, and in his autobiography he quotes the following words from *The Dynasts*: 'War makes rattling good history; but peace is poor reading.'[7]

The solemnity of his demeanour furnished an ideal backcloth for his humour that was as alive as it was dead-pan. At a Pilgrims' Dinner for Lord Harlech he spoke of the excellence of his performance as Ambassador in Washington. No doubt a different criterion applied in the diplomatic service from that in the army. During his service in the army during the war he had learnt that the report 'Very good', written at the conclusion of a man's lifetime of service, meant that he had not been convicted of any crime.

Lunching with him one day at London airport to the sound of aeroplane engines and the smell of kerosene, I mentioned a report produced by a group of scientists who had asked for an

---

7 Stewart, *Life and Labour*, p. 178.

interview. I suggested that I should try and put them off with a brief letter of thanks. 'You can try it on,' Stewart said, 'but I don't think that it will satisfy them.'

'Oh, then you know the group?' I asked. 'No; but I know human nature.'

I laughed, and he added that obviously people who had gone to the trouble to produce a report would not be fobbed off all that easily.

On another occasion I was saying to Stewart that some Foreign Minister who had asked him to visit his country was very touchy.

'Yes,' Stewart replied, pensively adding, 'but what Foreign Minister is not touchy?'

Michael Stewart and his wife took the Soviet Foreign Minister and Mrs Gromyko to *Othello* at the National Theatre. They were received in the interval by the Queen Mother, who happened to be at the theatre for the same performance. After the play was over Mrs Stewart asked Mrs Gromyko if she liked it. 'Yes,' she said, 'but the performance I liked best was meeting the Queen. She's like a real queen, isn't she?'

One of the Foreign Secretary's responsibilities is to accompany the Queen on foreign visits. At the outset of Her Majesty's journey to the Federal Republic of Germany in 1965, he was conscientiously worried whether his participation could really add anything, but he came to enter into the spirit of it. He was amused by the hesitancy of photographers in the crowd who, having taken the Queen's car, looked up and wondered whether it was worth wasting film on the vehicle carrying him; or by the delayed exclamations of '*schön*' or '*entzückend*' which, having missed the correct target, were wafted through the window of his car.

We left the party at Bonn to rejoin it some days later in Berlin. The Queen's reception there was rapturous. It was a day of driving through a tunnel of applauding faces. There was an assortment of improvised posters, such as '*Wir grüssen die Königin*'. One, I noticed, ran proudly, 'God save the Queer'.[8]

The climax of the Berlin visit came outside the Rathaus where there were thousands of cheering children. The Queen was due to speak, but they would not stop shouting. They chanted 'Eliz-a-beth' louder and louder whenever anyone tried to stop them. The Queen seemed rather nervous, but she got through the speech, which was then put into German, through further prolonged applause.

From 5 p.m. to midnight that same day, the Monarch did Hannover: a tour of the town; the signing of yet another Golden Book; the handing over of another inkstand; then the return to the train which had served as a home for the Royal Family and entourage since Bonn; quick change into evening dress and drive to Herrenhaus for a banquet and reception followed by fireworks; and finally back to the train through cheering torch-lit crowds to join the suite for a midnight drink in the bar of the train.

The train was a marvel, longer, we were told, than any other in Germany. It spent the night in sidings and had to be broken up to fit into them. Sometimes it was made up the following day in a different order, which confused those marching down the corridor to breakfast. Breakfast was an outrageously English affair,

---

8 Michael Stewart enjoyed misprints. I drew his attention to a German one, 'Roast bastard and mushed potatoes'. He said that he had seen a menu somewhere boasting 'Toad and Mould'.

served, for everyone except for the Royal Family, in the long din-ing-car, with fried eggs, marmalade, toast and coffee and the lat-est English newspapers. These were flown out each morning from London, and the pilot managed to find the train wherever it was.

The nights in sidings presented one problem: the lavatories had injunctions in several languages but particularly peremptory in German, about *nicht* using them while the train was stationary. The suite became less and less sensitive to this as the week wore on. One morning when Martin Charteris[9] emerged from the lavatory, there was an enormous German guard standing outside. Martin apologized, saying he had been unable to wait. 'That doesn't matter,' the German said, 'it is only a very small station.'

Our departure from Hamburg was dramatic. The whole party toured the port in launches before going aboard *Britannia*, tied up right in the middle of the city, dark blue new paint all over and very shiny. The Queen received a number of dignitaries in the lounge. She then gave photographs and decorations to members of the British staff stationed in Germany who had helped with the arrangements. It was all done very discreetly. They queued up in predetermined order, were announced by Lord Plunket[10] and then received in a special cabin where, I was told, the Queen does all her signings and presentations. Then the banquet on board for the Federal President and Chancellor. It was to start at 7.30 prompt and be all over by 8.30 exactly, so that we could catch the tide and sail at 9 p.m. Martin Charteris told me to watch out for the speedy service. There was nothing like it. Whizz, flip, and it

---

9 Lord Charteris, Private Secretary to the Queen and later Provost of Eton.
10 Lord Plunket, Equerry to the Queen.

would all be over and cleared away, speeches and all. This was certainly what happened. There seemed to be one steward for each of the fifty guests and the courses were served at a breakneck pace.

The next morning, with quite a sea running, Michael Stewart asked me to arrange for him to be shown over the ship. So we went up and down gangways and in and out of engine and wardrooms, meeting many of the people at work on *Britannia*. I felt quite queasy at the end of it. I told Martin Charteris so, just as we were about to go in to lunch. 'Well, you can do anything on this ship, old boy,' he said, 'but you mustn't actually be sick in front of the Queen.' I hadn't until then thought of such an awful prospect, but once the idea had been inserted into my head, I became convinced that if I went into lunch I would be bound to commit the one unforgivable sin. So I withdrew from the party. When later I was taking the air on deck, I passed the Duke of Edinburgh pacing up and down. 'I never make any bones about it,' he said in friendly fashion. 'For the first twenty-four hours at sea I take a pill, otherwise I feel it.'

We were looked after beautifully on board, never allowed to feel out of it and made to feel particularly at home in the Equerries' Room where Martin Charteris, Squadron-Leader Checketts, the Duke of Edinburgh's Equerry, and the ladies-in-waiting, Lady Leicester and Lady Susan Hussey, managed by the informality of their language and anecdotes to banish any semblance of stuffiness. It was a treat for me to have been a guest on *Britannia*. The maintenance of good relations with the Palace is certainly part of the unwritten code of responsibility of the Foreign Office Private Office, no less important than keeping in good repair the links with the other Private Offices in Whitehall. With Martin Charteris serving as the Private Secretary to the Queen at this time, connections between us and the Palace were serenely unencumbered.

Not long afterwards Michael Stewart had to go on a trip to the United States. I asked him whether he would want to give a dinner party on our one night in New York on the way back from Washington. U Thant would not be able to come, but he would be seeing him for drinks beforehand. Aware that the paperwork would have been piling up, as he remained in charge of the Office even when abroad, I suggested that he might like to avoid any dinner commitments so as to cope with the boxes. I added, betraying I suppose a lack of psychological insight, that I was sure he would be very tired by then.

'If I am,' he said, 'that is something that will have to be dealt with. But I don't think I can spend the night in New York dining alone in the hotel.' So he had a dinner in the Carlyle Hotel, with a mixture of guests including the President of the UN General Assembly and the Chairman of the New York Stock Exchange.

I give the day's programme below to show the sort of pace these foreign journeys entailed (I am sure they are no less strenuous nowadays):

06.15   Called by Washington Embassy valet.
07.00   Breakfast with Robert Macnamara.
08.30   Delegation meeting in the Chancery.
09.30   Meeting at the State Department with George Ball.
10.30   Meeting at the State Department with Dean Rusk.
11.30   Meeting with the President at the White House.

13.15   Speech at Press Club, followed by questions (audience of several hundred leading journalists).

14.15   Lunch at Press Club.

14.45   Delegation meeting in the British Embassy to clear telegrams to London and sign letters.

15.00   Press Conference for British Press at the British Embassy.

15.30   Leave Embassy for airport.

17.15   Arrive by air at New York and drive straight to UN headquarters.

18.00   Meeting with U Thant.

19.15   Press Conference at UN building.

20.15   Dinner at Carlyle Hotel.

23.15   Read telegrams from London and approve outgoing ones.

23.45   Bed.

A few months after I had begun working as Private Secretary to Michael Stewart I ran into Arthur Drew, a senior civil servant. He said that he had been an almost exact contemporary of Stewart's at school. He had been a remarkable boy. He converted practically the whole school to Sinn Fein by the quiet passion of his advocacy. He had refused to join the OTC – he was almost the only boy to do so – and his objection was based on some principle other than pacifism. Drew implied that Michael Stewart was very much the same sort of person between 16 and 18 years of age as he was now, and one who inevitably won respect without in the least seeking it. The masters at the Blue-Coat School were apparently in awe of this gentle, reasonable, single-minded boy.

I often found myself wondering why he had left schoolmastering for politics. His wife said one day on television that 'it was his heart which had taken him into politics'. She said she could not understand how anyone could think of her husband as heartless. From my own obviously much more limited observation, I felt sure that this was true. It explained partly why he was more of a success at the Foreign Office, dealing with human problems, than at the Department of Economic Affairs, handling economic planning. But I think that it was a wish to serve an essential cause by the use of his exceptional intellectual and forensic talents that had carried him into politics, as well as the promptings of his heart; and there was no doubt about his dedication to the Labour Party that must be defended and supported with utter loyalty, however much, on occasions, it might be wrong-headed.

Whilst avoiding the temptation to place the Foreign Secretaries I have known in some order of attainment, I cannot refrain from saying that I think Michael Stewart is one of the most underestimated, the result partly of his unassuming personality. Members of the Foreign Service have every reason to be grateful for the trust he placed in them. He had to contend, particularly in his first term as Foreign Secretary, with bitter opposition from the left wing of his own Party, but he never flinched. Given our economic weakness, the shadow of Vietnam and the distraction of many residual problems of Empire, e.g. Gibraltar and the Falklands, I do not think that Michael Stewart could at that time have stamped British foreign policy with any definite and enduring mark or achievement. But by the strength of reason, in which he so ardently believed, and by his integrity, so evident to all who dealt with him, he managed to prevent many disasters that might have befallen us – a serious deterioration in relations with the USA as a result of Vietnam, or the setting of a dangerous precedent for Africa had he equivocated over Biafra.

It was a hard stroke of fate that the policy and style that Michael Stewart brought to Labour's foreign policy should not have had a chance in government in the fifties when they might have helped to bring about the long-overdue adjustment and commitment of resources necessary to establish our proper position in the world.

The Personnel Department of the FCO decided in the summer of 1965 that I had been long enough in London (six years) and that it was time I was posted abroad again. I was sent to Madrid. So ended the second of my spells in the Private Office.

9

WHITEHALL AND
HOMO POLITICUS

Twenty years have passed since I worked in the Private Office, yet in the interval, largely spent in foreign posts, I have frequently been made aware of the importance of that Office, no less pivotal to those serving abroad than to those at home. Other Ministerial Private Offices in London, particularly at No. 10, have also at times been equally important to me when overseas. If I wished to know the pulse of Whitehall, I found that I had to keep in touch with the Private Secretaries, not regularly, but when the pressure seemed to be changing one way or another.

Although I am aware how specific examples can easily distort a general theme, I nevertheless think that one or two will help to illustrate my meaning. By the late seventies, British industry seemed to be in a state of almost irreversible decline and those of us representing the country abroad were conscious of the effect of this upon British interests. In Paris, I wondered whether there was anything that could usefully be done about it, and decided that every effort should be made to secure Britain's return to the European Airbus consortium from which we had withdrawn in the late sixties. Rather than become a minor partner of an American aircraft producer, for example Boeings, which was one alternative, we should try to remain important airframe producers ourselves by joining with the European manufacturers, each of whom at that time was smaller than we were. We would be welcomed in and could secure reasonable terms such as might not be available to us again later. The pressure that I therefore exerted on London in this sense could well, as I realized, be grating in its effect and thus counter-productive, but I did not have much idea how it was going down. It is always difficult abroad to know whether anyone at home ever reads what you say or what the impact is. You do not receive, for instance, telegraphic instructions telling you to shut up, or at least I never did, though the sentiment may well have been there, and indeed it was – over the aeroplanes – in certain quarters in London. What I learned from the Private Offices which I got into touch with was that while I was certainly annoying certain people I should not on that account necessarily desist, but that I should, if I wanted it to be effective, reshape my argument in ways suggested to me that provided the necessary support for those at home, whether Ministers or officials, promoting the cause I was favouring.

Or a quite different example. When Tony Crosland was taken ill at the beginning of 1977 and had to be removed to hospital, his French opposite number was anxious to know how serious it was, both for personal reasons and because of the urgent business outstanding. He asked me to find out, upon which I telephoned the Private Secretary who left me in no doubt about the gravity of the Minister's condition, information that I was able to pass on to Monsieur Guiringaud.

Or a third and completely different illustration of the Private Office's importance to posts abroad. During the six months in 1980 when the British held the Presidency of the European Council of Ministers we were involved in initiatives affecting the Middle East. These were of acute concern to Washington, where I was then serving as Ambassador. My best, and indeed only, way of finding out what might be behind Europe's policies so as to be able to deal with American enquiries was to approach the Private Office of the Foreign Office for informal background material.

In another realm of activity, that of Ministerial visits which loom large in the life of ambassadors, particularly in major posts, and which were frequent during my time in Washington, there are many issues that can only be sorted out between the Private Office and the post abroad; for example, the personal likes and dislikes, including food and drink, of the Minister (for instance, David Owen disliked high flower arrangements in the dining-room; Peter Carrington did not want wine for himself at lunch); or the content of his programme and of his speeches. Several of his Private Secretaries normally accompany the Foreign Secretary on his journey and, rather like an invading army, they will try to establish themselves and set up something in the nature of a Private Office in the Embassy. I have seen many such expeditions come and go with the force and rapidity of a typhoon, leaving nothing behind except signed photographs and a sense of relief amongst those briefly occupied.

In the preface to the earlier edition, I mentioned the significance of the network of Private Offices in Whitehall for the general conduct of the Government's business. It is one of the means by which the policies of the different Departments of State are co-ordinated. Serving abroad for a number of years has only confirmed me in my view of the importance of this close mesh, a system that does not exist to a like degree anywhere else, so far as I have seen. At a small lunch party given by John Egremont, who was Macmillan's Private Secretary for many years, I heard Macmillan giving his views on the role of the Private Secretary in the British system of government. 'If you want to get anything done in government,' Macmillan said, with a theatrical pause, 'it's no good going to the top. It only antagonizes the officials. You have to know someone who knows someone who really does the job. I remember when I was in North Africa during the war, if I wanted a special aircraft it was no good my asking the Commander-in-Chief. He would have said no, and muttered something about the rules. But if I asked my Private Secretary, he would have talked on an old-boy basis to his opposite number and the whole thing would have been fixed up.'

Of course there is more to it than the fixing of transport. A Minister may often wish, before considering some new policy or some proposal for eventual submission to the Cabinet, to know how it will be viewed by one of his Ministerial colleagues and the latter's department. He may, of course, have a chance to ask the Minister himself. But often he will leave it to his Private Office to find out how the wind sits in other quarters of Whitehall, particularly at No. 10. One of the Private Secretaries has the responsibility for preparing the Minister for Cabinet. This is no mean task, getting together the papers and the briefs, which, however little they may have to do with foreign affairs, can have much to do with the Minister's political obligations.

The relationship between members of the Private Office and

their opposite numbers at No. 10 is subtle and complex. It is in part, but only in part, a reflection of relations between the Prime Minister and the Foreign Secretary. During my time these reached their apotheosis in the absolute confidence that existed between Attlee and Bevin. 'If you have a good dog, don't bark yourself,' wrote Attlee in his autobiography, '... and in Bevin I had an exceptionally good dog.'[1] This meant of course that Bevin had masterly support in Cabinet.

A certain degree of irritation, actual or potential, between the Prime Minister and the Foreign Secretary is the normal law of Whitehall, as is latent tension between their Private Offices. Foreign Ministers, unless merely their Master's voice, are as little inclined to welcome interference from No. 10 as Prime Ministers are disinclined to resist the lure of playing *la grande politique* in the international arena. This built-in friction is apt to show itself on the surface in the small ways I have mentioned, such as the almost habitual dislike of Foreign Secretaries at having to attend on the PM at Chequers – symbol to them of the latter's superior status; or their customary ill humour when accompanying the PM on visits abroad, which is nevertheless nothing to their mood if there is any suggestion of their being left behind!

The members of the FO Private Office will not openly admit to any second-fiddle feelings *vis-à-vis* the Private Office at No. 10, whence nevertheless they are not accustomed to expect treatment on equal terms. Seconded from different departments of Whitehall and known for their competence and adaptability, it is amazing how quickly the Private Secretaries, once arrived at No. 10,

---

1 C. R. Attlee, *As It Happened*, p. 169.

come to adjust themselves to their new altitude. The senior ones manage to throw off all former diffidence of manner, the hallmark of the civil servant. They succeed effortlessly in rising above the narrow horizons of their parent departments. They often appear to find no difficulty in discarding the official mentality altogether and in identifying themselves with their political master, cursing the various Ministries and their entire staff of dry-as-dust neutrals. Not only are the senior officials throughout Whitehall treated authoritatively, but the members of the Cabinet are addressed on level terms – sometimes by Christian name just to show there's no disequilibrium. If they are nothing outside Whitehall, the top Private Secretaries at No. 10 are very important figures within that hidden yet imposing world. They have no political responsibility. They are not even accountable to any government department. But they have the ear and eye of the PM and that is enough to give them immense influence. No. 10 exercises so strong a metamorphosis that some who have been Private Secretaries there for long, finding it difficult, once their time there is up, to reverse the life-cycle and return to the departmental chrysalis whence they came, fly off to high posts in Whitehall or sometimes to the City – to the relief, it must be admitted, of their old departments, which may have been made to feel too humdrum, too plodding, to accommodate them.

These are the people with whom the Private Secretaries at the FO, displaying naturally no similar sense of superiority, and kept down to earth by an ever-watchful department, must remain on close terms if they are to provide for the Secretary of State the essential link with the Prime Minister. Although sensible to the charge of anti-climacticism in mentioning it, I have to record in all honesty that during my spells in the Private Office I was on the best of terms with Jock Colville and Oliver Wright at No. 10; they became life-long friends.

As suggested earlier, the Private Office network throughout Whitehall is, therefore, of value to Ministers in helping them to know what to expect from their colleagues when it comes to meetings. But once the Minister is in the Cabinet he is on his own. It is up to him alone how he does. Harold Caccia, who, after a long career at the heart of government, knew as well as anyone the sharp divide between politicians and officials, used to sum it up in characteristically sporting fashion: 'It's the man at the crease who counts, no matter how many wiseacres there are in the pavilion.' Perhaps the most the Private Secretary can do is to ensure that the Minister knows the feeling of the department on any issue. Nothing, except perhaps repeated failures of their Chief in the House of Commons, undermines the morale of the Office and the standing of the Minister in the department more than frequent defeats in the Cabinet on matters of close interest to them. But the Private Secretary will know, more than do the different sections of the Office, that the Secretary of State cannot be expected to win every time and that it will be counter-productive for him to be equally combative in Cabinet on all issues.

Attlee said something interesting to me once about his conduct of Cabinet meetings; it was at a small lunch Frank Longford gave for him in 1956 on the day he was to take his seat in the House of Lords. He had just been reading Philip Magnus's biography of Gladstone and he was astonished to find that Gladstone had been able to avoid having a Cabinet meeting sometimes for as long as three months on end. Attlee clearly envied him in this respect. But he explained how he had evolved a way of getting through Cabinet meetings with the minimum delay. He had always begun by praising the paper under discussion, and would then say, turning to the Minister who had signed it, that he presumed he did not wish to add anything to so excellent a presentation of the case. 'That usually silenced him,' Attlee said in his clipped style. He went on to say that his next step in Cabinet was not to enquire whether everyone agreed with the paper, since this would have been asking for trouble, but to move rapidly to a conclusion by saying, 'Well, if no one has any objection, we'll let that go.'

Attlee was full of this kind of practical wisdom which in someone more worldly might have been taken for cynicism. I heard him once throw away another remark which suggested much cold calculation beneath the surface. It occurred over a glass of sherry before lunch. Someone, an Englishman, needless to say, was saying that he could never get excited about US politics. Both sides seemed to stand for the same thing. 'What on earth,' he asked, somewhat monotonously waxing to his theme, 'what in God's name is the difference between the Republicans and Democrats?' Taking a sip of dry sherry, Attlee replied monosyllabically, 'Jobs. That's what it is, jobs.'

I mentioned earlier the two-way nature of the Private Secretary's loyalty and obligation. He does not merely make the Minister's wishes about policy known to the department (and to posts abroad) but he is responsible for ensuring that the views of the Office (and of Ambassadors) are fully brought to the attention of the Minister. This may be a ticklish business. He may be asked for his personal opinion about the suitability of a certain appoint-

ment; where there is a conflict of view within the Office he may
be expected to express a preference; or even where there is a
unanimous submission, supported by the Permanent
Under-Secretary, he may be asked whether he thinks that the Secretary of State should go along with it despite the doubtful political implications. If the Private Secretary automatically sides with
the recommendation made by the Office even when the Secretary
of State has doubts, and he does so without any convincing or additional argument, he may lose his master's confidence. If, on the
other hand, he regularly and evidently opposes the Office's views,
he will come to be regarded as one-sided in his influence. He will
get across the Permanent Under-Secretary, who does after all bear
the responsibility. Harold Caccia, who served both as Permanent
Under-Secretary, and in earlier years as Assistant Private Secretary, castigated the members of the Private Office at the height
of some crisis as being like harlots, exercising power without
responsibility.

So the Private Secretary has a tightrope to walk; and the only
net beneath him is another, inevitably less exalted, post. The Secretary of State cannot save him from falling, if the department
refuse to co-operate with him in a way that makes his task of in-
termediary impossible. In picking his way, inevitably in somewhat feline fashion, between dangerous, criss-cross paths within
the Office, the Private Secretary always has at his disposal one re-
course that can be decisive: he can suggest to the Secretary of
State that he holds a meeting with all those representing contrasted views. At one time James Cable, who was Head of the
South East Asian Department, told me of his worry about a particular problem. He had submitted a recommendation but this

had been rejected by higher authority and never reached the Secretary of State. When a suitable opportunity occurred, I mentioned this to the Secretary of State because Cable seemed to me to have an *a priori* case to be heard. It was agreed that a meeting should be called and when this was held the whole problem was thrashed out. I do not recall what the outcome was but I do know that Cable and others felt that at least attention had been given to their views.

On another occasion Michael Butler told me that he thought we were getting into mounting difficulty in the confrontation between Malaysia and Indonesia. If the battle continued, it would be an increasingly dangerous and expensive operation. Whoever replaced Sukarno would be worse from our point of view. Communist influence was spreading. He thought that the whole issue should be looked at again to see whether we should either get a serious negotiation going or step up military action to obtain a solution that way. He had been unable to persuade senior officials to look at the problem afresh. They seemed to accept the impasse, not complacently but resignedly. Struck by the fact that an important defence review was taking place on the assumption that confrontation would still be with us in five years' time, an assumption that materially affected the whole defence programme, including the size of the British Army of the Rhine, and that took it for granted that we would still be conducting this military operation alone and not as part of an allied effort with the United States engaged, I suggested to the Secretary of State that I should do a minute on his behalf asking the Office to review the whole problem and how to end it. This instruction from the Secretary of State went to all those involved and led eventually to a thorough examination of the whole issue.

The Private Secretary should never get into a corner in which he is forced to answer the question: is this instruction from the Secretary of State himself, or have you been putting words into his mouth? It must always be assumed that anything emanating from the Private Office has the Secretary of State's sanction. This means that the Private Secretary must clear his lines in advance with the Secretary of State or be quite sure he will back him up if necessary. It also means that everything coming from the Private Office in the Secretary of State's name must be in character. Obviously it would be absurd if minutes were stemming from the Private Office containing views from the Secretary of State on subjects upon which he was known to have little knowledge or interest. Not surprisingly, Henry Kissinger in his book on his White House years has hit the nail on the head in describing the role of the presidential assistant. The authority of the assistant, he says, 'is like that of a trainer in a wild-animal act. His mastery depends on never being challenged.' It is the same with the Private Secretary in our system of government.

On the broad sweep of policy I did manage to inject one piece of expertise, or some prejudice, on a subject about which I felt strongly at the time. This was possible because it was so general, and so pervasive, that it did not really fall within the responsibility of any one department; and it was something so theoretical, so detached from the immediate interests of Britain in any particular field, that it had not come under the aegis of the Planners. The Secretary of State at the time had tended to accept the conventional view in London, and certainly the one held at the time by the United States Secretary of State, that the Soviet-Chinese conflict was primarily an ideological one; and a corollary of this was that the Soviets were seen as the 'good boys' seeking peaceful settlements, and the Chinese were regarded as the aggressors in word and deed; and it was assumed somehow that it was in the interests of the West to favour the Russians rather than the Chinese. I will not bother here to go into the reasons why I considered this a false line of argument. But what is relevant is that the Secretary of State came to see that deep interests of state, strategic and historical, rather than conflicts of ideology, were at stake between Peking and Moscow. It has to be said in all honesty however that the Secretary of State was much encouraged to change his mind by the information obliquely imparted to him that the black-and-white view of the Sino-Soviet relationship, the former seen as 'baddies' and the latter as 'goodies', was the favourite theme of the Secretary of State's predecessor. That finished it.

I have referred earlier to the uniqueness of the British system of the Private Office. In France and Germany, to take two countries where, in my view, the Private Secretary system operates differently, my impression is that the loyalty of the Directeur de Cabinet is much more to the Minister than to the department. He conveys policy downwards more than acting as a broker for the department with the Minister. This arises from the greater politicization of the Private Secretary. If not a known member of the Minister's Party, he will certainly be politically sympathetic to him and it would be rare for him to remain in the Office after a change of Ministers. Of course this is but a reflection of the different attitude in these two countries, compared with ours, towards civil servants and political affiliation. In Paris, for instance, an official can be known to belong to a Party without this being considered any impediment to his objectivity as a civil servant. (The same is true in the Federal Republic of Germany.) It does mean, however, that with a change of administration there is a shift in the top ranks of the machinery of government. In France any lack of continuity that this might produce is to some extent attenuated by the degree to which the administration, including of course the composition of Ministers' Cabinets, is dominated by former pupils of the Ecole Nationale d'Administration. These *Enarques*, as they are called, have come to be an élite that virtually runs France regardless of the Party in power; whatever their political complexion, they will, from training and discipline, see problems in the objective light of France's overall interests.

The French tend to think that with our method we do not get, after a change of government, the fresh drive and new initiatives in policy that a shift in political will should produce. Our system, they believe, generates monotony and inertia. Under their procedures there is no problem for Ministers in ensuring that their political direction extends to all those serving under them. The same sort of criticism has been made recently in this country with a suggestion that Ministers, particularly the Prime Minister, should bring people in from outside the Civil Service, to infuse the government with the necessary political drive and enthusiasm. There may be something in this idea for No. 10 and home departments. I can well understand, for instance, that Prime Ministers need senior advisers to be constantly on hand to look after their interests in various areas including foreign affairs. The Foreign Secretary is too busy attending to his own department and too often abroad attending conferences to be able to fill this role. The Prime Minister does in fact always have an official from the Foreign Office in the Private Office of No. 10. He should be able to meet the needs I have mentioned, but if not, there may well be a requirement for someone without any departmental allegiance or responsibilities. As regards home departments, I cannot speak with any authority; but obviously civil servants are not necessarily suited by training or background to run anything in the nature of a business. Whitehall may well be in need of innovation. The French seem to me to have devised a system of interchange between government and industry that has helped to transform the country's economy in the space of the last twenty-five years and that might well have some lessons for us.

I can imagine that the Minister of Labour, for instance, could wish that he had someone alongside him who was both politically committed and an expert on labour relations; civil servants are bound to be cautious and full of forebodings about change; they will naturally feel responsible for warning him of all the dire consequences that could follow such and such a radical change of policy. I can see too that a Foreign Secretary might want to get at the raw material of a problem before it has been through the official blender. For this he might yearn for a special expert adviser with sharp political antennae. But I cannot pretend that it is easy to introduce political advisers into the Foreign and Commonwealth Office. An outsider will not know thoroughly the Office machine, nor the people in it, nor those abroad. He is unlikely to be well instructed in the best way to win the in-fighting in Whitehall. He may well be subjected to the cold-shoulder of permanent officials. This was certainly the lot of Stuart Hampshire, the distinguished philosopher and later Warden of Wadham College, Oxford, who in his earlier days was recruited to a Ministerial office in the Foreign Office. I happened to see a circulation slip under which the Senior Private Secretary sent the incoming telegrams round to the members of the Private Office. He had crossed out Hampshire's name and had written against it 'NOT NECESSARY'. However, the normal Foreign Office tendency will be to embrace newcomers rather than to reject them, a bear-hug that may nevertheless be suffocating for the newcomer.

In my experience, Foreign Office officials are only too eager to carry out the wishes of their political masters. What they look for is a clear-cut lead. I am aware that they have frequently been criticized for belonging to a particular caste and inclining to one Party's point of view. Before World War II for instance Foreign Office officials were lumped together as right-wing and pro-Catholic, though in fact, with one or two exceptions, particularly Nevile Henderson in Berlin (no relation), they were resolutely anti-appeasement and by and large critical of the Prime Minister, Neville Chamberlain.

The charge of being establishment and anti-left-wing was again levelled at the time of the Labour governments in the sixties and seventies, and I remember a senior Minister protesting to me that Foreign Office officials considered issues, not from the objective standpoint of British interests, but from a 'framework of reference that is one-sided'. More recently Foreign Office officials have come in for condemnation from the right for being 'wet' and not standing up for Britain's interests in a sufficiently vigorous way. But I do not think that these passing breezes should be taken too seriously; certainly Bevin rejected them. I shall never forget the way he turned on left-wing members of his own Party for running down officials in the Foreign Office and called upon them to try attacking him rather than those who were working loyally for him.

David Owen has recently said in an interview with Simon Jenkins that when he was made Foreign Secretary he became aware on entering the Foreign Office of the fact that, quite unlike either the Ministry of Defence or the Department of Health, here was a very determined department who thought that their view was the right view. 'My problem with the Foreign Office came upon implementation because some, actually only a few, but unfortunately in rather important positions, would fight the implementation of a decision taken by the Secretary of State.' But whether seen from the Private Office or from posts abroad, the Foreign Office, so it has seemed to me, has suffered in recent decades, not from being too assertive or too politically biased, but from being afraid to give advice for fear of being accused of the sort of tendencies David Owen has mentioned. They are apt to fudge issues. With the important exception of David Owen, I do not know of any Secretary of State who has served any length of time in the Office who maintains that he has been thwarted by the obstruction of his officials. Of course, I am assuming a certain degree of bipartisanship in foreign policy such as has prevailed since World War II. Suez imposed a severe strain upon the code of loyal service to political masters, and the same would, I think, apply if a future government were to adopt an extremely radical policy, such as withdrawal from the European Community or from NATO.

My conclusion on this complicated matter is that if alternating tides at the polls fail to bring about a corresponding reinvigoration and redirection of foreign policy, the remedy surely lies with the politicians elected to create and guide policy.

Finally, work in the Private Office provides a unique insight into the nature of *homo politicus*, a species rare and extraordinary to those who watch from afar. Apart from close proximity to Ministers in his own government, the Private Secretary, thanks to his attendance at the international meetings, will have the chance to observe the political leaders of the world.[2] The formal discussions themselves are often dull in substance, each side repeating its well-known points of view, but there is plenty of opportunity, on and offstage, to study the personalities and reactions of the politicians. Not only is the individual leader under long exposure, but politicians as a species come so sharply into focus that it is impossible to avoid leaping to certain conclusions about them. 'What is it', the Private Secretary will find himself wondering, 'that the Foreign Minister seated the other side of the table has that his fellow citizens do not possess? Why is he in power? How is it that this man over there, not noticeably distinguished in personality or intellect, should have come to be the chosen representative of his country at this important international gathering?' The Private Secretary, looking round the table, may not be able to suppress the disrespectful thought that were a stranger suddenly to be wafted into the meeting, he would not inevitably be impressed by the conduct of the proceedings or the performance of the actors. He would be unlikely automatically to be awe-struck or say to himself, 'These are outstanding men'. International

---

2 At the risk of name-dropping, but to illustrate the point, may I list the following Russians and Americans from among the many foreign statesmen I was able to observe at close quarters through the peep-hole of the Private Office: Stalin, Molotov, Vyshinsky, Khrushchev, Gromyko, Truman, Byrnes, Acheson, Johnson, Rusk and Macnamara.

conferences are nearly always dull, and politicians are by no means always dazzling, particularly when they are away from their home ground. They are not invariably eloquent or profound or far-sighted. They do not appear to be, and may not in fact be necessarily more patriotic or public-spirited than many of their compatriots in other careers. Not all of them appear abroad as even typical of the people they represent. Their clarity of conscience, to which they sometimes allude with pride, may to others seem opaque. Few are inspired by any lofty and original philosophy of government – at any rate for long. Mature and worldly men, they are not unfailingly possessed with that personal magnetism which could make them stand out, as it does certain boys in their school-days, as indubitable leaders of men. They are not – and this is the last but perhaps not least surprising of the negative generalizations to be made here about politicians the world over on the basis of my own experience – they are not men who have been impelled on this frequently disappointing and invariably demanding career uniquely by private ambition.

What then are the positive features which, to the outsider, tend to be common to politicians? For after all they have forced their way to the top by certain strong qualities. They would not be there in the modern world purely by inheritance or privilege. Regardless of frontiers they do seem to share certain traits: physical toughness, self-assurance, and capability. There was a famous occasion when a group of British MPs visiting the USSR had an interview with Khrushchev. After he had held forth for some time, one of them said to him rather patronizingly that it was clear that the First Secretary was a man of wide knowledge and great capacity for governing his country. 'Do not be surprised,' Khrushchev retorted angrily, 'I would not be the ruler of two hundred million tough and dynamic people were I not a person of exceptional ability.' Apropos of Khrushchev, I have to interject that when he was kicked out in October 1964, I was Private Secretary to R. A. Butler, having previously been Head of the Northern Department, which dealt with the Soviet Union. I was asked, I cannot remember by whom but it may well have been by Rab, if I had been taken unawares over this dismissal, and if so, why; to which I could only reply that, since Khrushchev himself had not foreseen it, I could hardly have been expected to have done so.

The talents I have listed above would not necessarily mark out a politician. They are not enough by themselves, and they are not unique to politicians. I realize the risk of making generalizations on such a matter and I am sure that the impulses that drive people into politics are manifold. In former times, for instance, family tradition may have been among them; and today a certain longing for collective acclaim and even love ('my constituents love me') may lure people through the gate of public life. But I believe that there are certain characteristics that anyone must possess in a high degree if he is to enter public life and survive there.

First, he must have a liking for publicity. He must enjoy appearing on platforms and television. He must be eager to make speeches. Officials are apt to think it a strain on their Minister if he has to make several speeches in a day; but in fact to a born and practised politician it is the breath of life. Bevin used to say that for him public speaking was no harder than breathing. The yearning for publicity is different from ambition, which can be fulfilled inconspicuously but adequately in many other walks of life. It was a favourite theme of Hugh Gaitskell's that what differentiated politicians above all from other men was the love of limelight, and Gaitskell was a strikingly self-analytical politician. Disraeli, who was certainly one of the most self-conscious of politicians, showed that he thought likewise when he said to John Bright one day in the House of Commons: 'We came here for fame.'

From my earliest days in the Private Office I came to realize how another characteristic often to be found in politicians, a highly developed sense of jealousy, can combine with this love of limelight to complicate international negotiations. Within hours of becoming Foreign Secretary, Bevin was complaining to the members of his Private Office at the Potsdam Conference about the way his American opposite number, Jimmie Byrnes, was trying to 'hog the limelight', to use Bevin's own expression. Each Minister wanted to secure the credit for any break in the deadlock and any solution that might be achieved, and they certainly wanted to stop the others collaring it. This is part of a general problem that dogs diplomacy: Ministers naturally seek to claim that it is they who have triumphed and the others who have yielded in some negotiation, a temptation which, however helpful to them domestically at the time, is likely to redound to their disadvantage when the next negotiation takes place.

There are exceptions to the limelight rule – politicians such as Attlee, Douglas-Home, Michael Stewart or Peter Carrington, who were clearly not drawn into public life primarily by love of publicity. For them, as for many others no doubt, it is a secondary impulse. They are governed principally by another essential ingredient in the make-up of a politician, one that they themselves might well be inhibited from expressing: a yearning for personal power for the sake of the public good. He must have a social conscience and he must believe that he can make a distinct contribution to the government of his country. He has to feel a sense of public mission with which his own personal ambition can be identified. If fame had been enough in itself he could have sought fulfilment in other ways. He is imbued, though he may shrink from saying it, with a sense of duty.

Yet people in other professions – the Civil Service, the Armed Forces, medicine, the Church, or teaching, for instance – are also motivated in varying degrees by public spirit; they are not in it just to make money or promote their personal interests. They too have power to affect the lives of others. What distinguishes most politicians is that their grail is a public one: it is not just public service, but service in public.

How far a politician will achieve this happy harmony of service both to the public and himself, will depend of course a great deal upon events outside his control. There is nothing constant or predictable about it. But one thing is certain: few can hope to succeed who do not combine in their person an instinct for power, a sense of public responsibility and a love of fame. At any rate, this is how it has looked from my seat in the wings of the international stage, wearing the convenient but inconspicuous colours of the Private Office.

It is not, however, the recollection of political motivation, the silhouette of any one personality, or the drama of any particular event that impresses itself most on the retina of my memory as the Private Office flickers in the mind's eye, but the features of that vast room and the awesomeness, however unacknowledged by us Private Secretaries at the time, of our no less vast responsibilities: the high-ceilinged expanse of the Private Office, encumbered by the paraphernalia of the past and by the immediate flow of boxes and telegrams and by a procession of visitors, many of them clamouring to impart 'just one word into the Secretary of State's ear'; and the presence hard by, through the heavy swing door, of the Secretary of State himself, the embodiment in retrospect more of abstract political power than of any individual personality, seated in the middle of an even larger room, its windows giving on to the Horse Guards and St James's Park, a view lit in the distance by the lights of Carlton House Terrace twinkling through the willow trees, and highlighted in the foreground by the pelicans, flapping and opening their enormous beaks, as if conducting the orchestra of lesser birds on the lake; and, suffusing the whole place, that sense of self-importance without obtrusiveness, of clandestinity, and, dare I say, of service, that inspires the go-between in all of us (except in those, and few they are, who lack both vanity and the desire to please), a quality that is as vital as is oxygen to the survival of life in the rarefied atmosphere of the Private Office.

EPILOGUE

In the two decades that have passed since I finished the original version of *The Private Office*, seven new Private Secretaries have served seven new Foreign Secretaries. I have compared their experiences in that office with mine and have learnt about their views on the interplay between Ministers and officials and on how far they agree with my interpretation of the nature of *homo politicus* as seen from nearby.

To start with the scenery, the décor of the Private Secretaries' room has changed and is no longer as shabby and stale as the stage-set of Agatha Christie's *Mousetrap*. Photographs or prints of all Foreign Secretaries hang in sequence round the walls, starting with the first, Charles James Fox. Modern technology is conspicuous: computers glare down on every desk; a TV set protrudes from high up in one corner. Boxes, red, black, and brown, which used to be piled high on a central table like children's bricks, are now kept in their place in a specially constructed whatnot. The room has a less clubland and a more business-like feel about it than in my day.

The Foreign Secretary's room in 1984.

The Secretary of State's room, the grandest of all Ministerial offices, did not under Robin Cook's[1] regime enjoy Derry Irvinesque[2] attention or display any frills. The portrait of a Nepalese Prince, bearing a curved sword, which had long hung above the fireplace, had been replaced, initially by a mirror, and then by a

1 The Rt. Hon. Robin Cook, MP, Secretary of State for Foreign and Commonwealth Affairs, 1997–2001.
2 Irvine of Lairg, Baron, appointed Lord High Chancellor of Britain in 1997.

painting by John Bratby featuring prominently a packet of corn-flakes. The other painting introduced by Robin Cook, a lover of the turf, was a scene from Newmarket. A bust of Ernest Bevin stood one side of the fireplace on a disproportionately large white plinth; a TV set graced the other side. Robin Cook replaced the Hansard reports in the large cabinet on one wall by examples of British invention and design; among them, a wind-up radio, a device for shrinking maps, a Harry Potter book, and a segmented nut replacement for Airbus. Photographs of the Queen and Prince Philip were displayed on a cabinet behind the Foreign Secretary's desk. A personal touch was provided by a stuffed ferret which adorned a nearby table. With the departure of Cook and the arrival of the new Foreign Secretary, Jack Straw, the array of British ingenuity in the display cabinet disappeared, as did the ferret. At the time of writing it is too early to say with what taxi-dermied creature or other keepsake the new Foreign Secretary will embellish the room.

The greatly increased presence of special advisers to ministers has inevitably made a considerable impact on the system of government and on the work of the Private Office. It has not, however, led to any more transparency about the central role in government of the Private Office, perhaps on account of the reticence of ministers and officials on the subject, for reasons I have suggested in the Prologue. As I have said there, this obscurity does not necessarily impair the work of the FCO, but it does hinder those later who try to reconstruct the rationale for policy decisions.

But, first, a word or two about the present day plethora of political advisers, and to what extent they are justified, as seen from the angle of a career civil servant. It depends, of course, on their number. It also varies from one office to another. I cannot speak for No. 10 or other government departments, but, as regards the FCO, I believe that the Foreign Secretary's need for political advisers is understandable for several reasons: the amount he has to travel out of the country; the enhanced involvement of public opinion in foreign issues; the speed and increased volume of communications and the demand for a rapid reaction or response; the absence of the former bipartisanship in foreign policy; and the watch that must be kept on the friendly attentions of his political rivals.

Advisers may not always find it easy to adapt to the ways of Whitehall, but I have the impression that officials in the FCO have come to accept their presence and requirements more readily than they did a generation ago.

After the original publication of *The Private Office* James Callaghan, in a generous letter to me, wrote that the FCO did not take enough notice of Ministers' relations with Parliament. I think his criticism was justified. His Private Office, he wrote, 'was usually forgetful (not obstructive) of the fact that I might want to go to listen to PM's Questions, or attend part of a debate. But to be around the place is part of a politician's source of strength and influence'. That partly explained, he went on, 'why Foreign Secretaries in the Lords are not a success when trouble blows up'.

The presence within, or on the fringes of, the Private Office of political advisers, does not, in my view, mean that the Private Secretary, being a civil servant, should be expected to be without political awareness or influence. Needless to say, he or she does not have to bear or acquire a party political label. Politicians in this country are not given to wishing to know the political allegiance of their civil servants, including private secretaries; and the latter do not feel under any obligation or pressure to incline to the Minister's party. I know that, when George Walden[3] was being considered for appointment to the Private Office under David Owen[4], he asked for the Minister to be left in no doubt that he was not a Labour supporter. Sherard Cowper-Coles[5], who was Private Secretary to Robin Cook, has told me that the question of his political affiliation never arose with the Minister any more than it did for anyone else in the Department.

I do not think, however, that you can draw a hard and fast line between official and political responsibilities and assume that a private secretary, because he is a civil servant, is some sort of political eunuch. The degree to which a Minister succeeds in some policy enterprise, in which the private secretary has inherently and officially been involved, will inevitably have repercussions on the Minister's political standing.

Recent evidence reinforces my earlier view that the sheer propinquity of the private secretary and the fact that he is with the Minister by day and often for most of the night means that, if confidence has been established between them, they are bound to discuss everything, personal, official and political. They travel the world together and there is nothing like travel for removing inhibitions. When Len Applyard[6], who had served in China and spoke

---

3 George Walden, CMG, Principal Private Secretary, 1978–81.
4 The Rt. Hon. Baron Owen, Secretary of State for Foreign and Commonwealth Affairs, 1977–9.
5 Sherard Cowper-Coles, Principal Private Secretary, 1999–2001.
6 Sir Leonard Appleyard, KCMG, Principal Private Secretary, 1984–6.

Mandarin, was Private Secretary to Geoffrey Howe[7] they spent much time going between London and Beijing. Howe, never a skimmer over the surface of problems, found himself during these journeys relying deeply on his Private Secretary's expertise on Hong Kong and China.

In his memoirs, *Conflict of Loyalty*, Howe related a personal decision he took that had important consequences not only for him but for the government more generally. The Department submitted two candidates to him from which to choose his Principal Private Secretary, giving preference to Charles Powell[8] over Len Appleyard. Of the two Howe knew Appleyard much the better and chose him. Powell was then made Private Secretary at No. 10 to Mrs Thatcher whom he proceeded to serve well – 'perhaps too well' according to Howe in his memoirs.

The Private Secretary to Geoffrey Howe needed exceptional stamina to survive and to record his innumerable ministerial meetings. It did not make it easy that Howe could do with not more than four hours sleep a night. In his last twelve months as Foreign Secretary he attended twenty-three meetings of European Ministers. To give another example: Howe had fifteen meetings with Eduard Shevardnadze, the Soviet Foreign Minister, one of which lasted for five hours.

I was struck by a passage in John Major's autobiography[9] which illustrates the inherent intimacy and confidence that de-

---

7 The Rt. Hon. Baron Howe, Secretary of State for Foreign and Commonwealth Affairs, 1983–9, published *Conflict of Loyalty,* Macmillan, 1994.
8 Lord Powell of Bayswater, member of the Diplomatic Service, Private Secretary to the Prime Minister 1983–91.
9 The Rt. Hon. John Major, *The Autobiography,* Harper Collins, 1999, p. 330.

velops in the Private Office – the unreality of supposing that there can be a Chinese wall separating political from official life. Stephen Wall[10], who had been Major's Principal Private Secretary at the FCO, joined him at No. 10 when he became Prime Minister. At the time of the Black Wednesday financial crisis in 1992 Major was so upset that he seriously considered resigning. 'I sought a dispassionate view from Stephen Wall, whom I knew well and trusted,' he wrote, adding that Wall advised strongly against and refused even to read a draft speech of resignation that Major had drafted. Wall had no inhibition about giving advice that was outside the realm of official duty any more than Major had had in asking for it.

A private secretary may well act in sympathy with a minister's objectives, going beyond the call of official duty, but without this amounting to political complicity. David Owen sensed that Stephen Wall, who was then his Assistant Private Secretary at the FCO, had a particular understanding of what he, Owen, was trying to achieve in Africa. He decided to make use of him in a way that went beyond normal private secretarial practice and he sent him on personal missions to Africa, Wall was, he said 'the best private secretary I ever had'[11].

In his memoirs[12] Owen recounts another occasion when, in 1977, Wall drew his attention, which the department had not done, to the 'evidence that the Argentines were taking an

---

10 Sir Stephen Wall, KCMG, Assistant Private Secretary 1977–9, and Principal Private Secretary 1988–9, to the Foreign Secretary, Foreign Affairs Adviser to the Prime Minister, 1991–3.

11 Kenneth Harris, *David Owen*, Weidenfeld & Nicolson, 1987, p. 190.

12 David Owen, *Time to Declare*, Michael Joseph, 1991, p. 357.

increasingly militant attitude'. This led him to call for a Ministerial re-examination of the problem which resulted in a decision to send a task force comprising a nuclear-powered submarine and two frigates to the Falkland Islands. Uncertainty exists about the impact of this decision. It had been decided that the despatch of the force should remain covert, and the Franks Review[13] 'found no evidence that the Argentine Government ever came to know of its existence'. But there is no doubt that the Argentine threat receded and that the resumed negotiations went reasonably well. David Owen drew the conclusion that it had not only been an example of 'how a politician can be the grit in the system, questioning and probing', but it had also shown how vital it was that the Private Office should be constantly alert. 'I often wondered', he wrote in reflective mood, ' what would have happened had I not queried Stephen Wall and if he had not used the word militant to me.'

It is the custom for the Foreign Secretary to deliver a speech at annual party conferences. Obviously the political adviser will be closely involved, but the Private Secretary is bound to contribute much of what the Minister has to say about the conduct of policy over the previous year. Again, politics will be inextricably linked with official business.

Helping with speeches is one of the Private Secretary's most demanding and, as I have indicated in the account of my time in the Private Office, one of his most trying tasks. Even if the Minister insists that in the end he has to do the actual drafting himself,

---

13 *Falkland Islands Review: Report of a Committee of Privy Counsellors*, Chairman, The Rt. Hon. The Lord Franks, January 1983, Cmnd. 8787, see Prologue above p xv.

he will require the Private Secretary to provide a lot of the basic material, and – more nerve-wracking – to hear his lines in advance. The Minister may on occasion use a telling phrase that an official has suggested, for example, about the inexpediency of 'megaphone diplomacy' (George Walden); or the danger of reliance on Star Wars as a 'Maginot Line' in space (Len Appleyard). These may well redound to the Minister's political credit.

If the Private Secretary becomes too political, and above all if this becomes publicized, it will be a mistake, blurring the constitutional divide between ministers and civil servants. This happened when Charles Powell was Private Secretary to Mrs Thatcher at No. 10. Percy Cradock, whom I have already mentioned, has written: 'It was sometimes difficult to establish where Mrs Thatcher ended and Charles Powell began. Perhaps it could be said that for some years he held the pen ... these abilities and activities, however, did not entirely accord with civil service norms. For example, Charles frequently overstepped the line between the official and political domain. He also had a flair for publicity. The rule was, and is, that private secretaries should be self-effacing and avoid the press. Charles on the other hand seemed to enjoy the most fruitful relations with them.'[14]

Without wishing to be too bland, I think one has to accept that Powell's conduct was a one-off. Whatever the annoyance it caused to the Foreign Office, the Foreign Secretary, and the Secretary to the Cabinet, however much it complicated Percy Cradock's task, and notwithstanding its conflict with norms, Powell indubitably served Mrs Thatcher superbly. Despite many

---

14 Sir Percy Cradock, *In Pursuit of British Interests*, pp. 14–15.

efforts to remove him she would not let him go. He was masterly at the job – as she had defined it, and as he, courageously in the face of the hostility of the rest of Whitehall, was prepared to carry it out. But he hardly serves as a model for a modern major Private Secretary. However, there is little chance, surely, of there being another just like him and another just like Mrs Thatcher in those offices at the same time.

Geoffrey Howe at the Foreign Office probably resented Charles at No. 10 more than anyone did. As his memoirs[15] reveal, when he was Foreign Secretary he was sensitive to the contribution, both good and bad, that could be made by contacts between the FCO Private Office and the Private Office at No. 10. This became all the more evident when relations between the principals were strained, as they were in his time. I have learnt that at a moment when tension was particularly acute over policy towards Europe, it was Stephen Wall, the Principal Private Secretary at the FCO, rather than the Minister himself, who sent No. 10 a redraft of the famous Bruges speech, much of whose anti-European content had been drafted by Charles Powell, albeit in accordance with Mrs Thatcher's sentiments. Judged by results, this diplomatic ploy was not a success.

In his heady early days as Foreign Secretary, Robin Cook evidently took insufficient account of the views of No. 10, not least those of Jonathan Powell[16], the head of the Private Office there. He decided to make morality the mainspring of his foreign policy. Michael Stewart had done much the same when he became

---

15 The Rt.Hon. Baron Howe, *Conflict of Loyalty,* Macmillan, 1994, see note p. 4.
16 Jonathan Powell, member of the Diplomatic Service, 1979–95, appointed Chief of Staff to the Prime Minister 1997.

Secretary of State a generation before. As I have already recounted, he believed that despite our continuing economic and political weakness we could and should set an example of good behaviour to the world. His homilies were mostly confined to a few officials in the Foreign Office who listened in polite but bemused silence; whereas Robin Cook decided to make an 'ethical content' a main public platform of his policy. It also formed a central theme of a much vaunted 'mission statement' by which all members of the Foreign Service were to be guided. He soon ran into difficulties over the export of arms. The demands of British trade and employment were incompatible with the zeal for an ethical dimension to policy decisions. According to Andrew Rawnsley[17], who was closer to the inside of New Labour than any outsider, at any rate until he blew the gaff on them, Jonathan Powell was furious at Cook's naïveté and simplistic approach. 'For days he could be heard wandering No. 10 spitting scorn about the Foreign Secretary. It was Powell ... not Cook who possessed the ear of the Prime Minister.' The Prime Minister chose soundness on commerce and jobs over ethics. More than a hundred licences were issued for the export of arms to Indonesia.

Earlier David Owen had pioneered a different application of ethics to foreign policy. A list of countries was drawn up in which they were ranked according to their human rights record. The degree of HMG's attention to each country was to depend on their humanitarian score reflected in this list. As the Private Secretary tactfully had to point out to his master, the trouble was that some,

---

17 Andrew Rawnsley, *Servants of the People: The Inside Story of New Labour,* Hamish Hamilton, 2000, p. 170.

or even many, of the countries with which we inextricably had to deal were those lowest down on the humanitarian ladder.

In his book *The Prime Minister*[18], Peter Hennessy opines that leading politicians are not by nature administrators, a generalization which many with whom I have spoken in preparing this epilogue consider would certainly apply to Tony Blair. They see him more as an evangelist. He wants things to happen but appears to have little idea how government works or to be guided by any enduring tenets, relying on rhetoric rather than follow-up action.

Hennessy makes Harold Wilson an exception to his generalisation. From my observation I think that Heath too took an interest in and understood administration. He wanted to move things along rather than just talk about them.

I also know of one instance which would justify an exception being made for Robin Cook. On becoming Foreign Secretary he was eager to extend the catchment area from which members of the Foreign Service were recruited. He therefore arranged for an open day to be held regularly at the Office to which he invited those who might have an influence on young people in the choice of a career. These presentations have been well attended and have been followed up by frequent visits to universities by the Permanent Under-Secretary of State (the PUS). The results have been staggering. The numbers of those applying to join the Foreign Service has multiplied, more people now wishing to join it than the Home Civil Service. Of the 4,500 candidates for entry to the Civil Service in the year 2000, 2,800 applied to join the Diplomatic Service (for which there were only twenty-five places). In

---

18 Peter Hennessy, *The Prime Minister*, Penguin, 2000.

the choice of careers by those leaving British universities the Diplomatic Service ranked top for the first time, outstripping the pull of the City, the BBC, industry or business. I do not know why this change should have occurred but it may reflect a shift in the focus of the present generation from materialism to public service and a greater global concern and interest. (In parenthesis I may add that members of the Diplomatic Service nowadays tend to stay on in the Service for their full time, whereas earlier the retention rate was low.)

I cannot resist interjecting here my personal view that what these developments reflect is that, notwithstanding the changes in Britain's relative standing in the world, and however transformed the means of communication and travel, the Diplomatic Service remains a great career; international relations is now a growth industry, and it is heartening that the young of today appear to be wise to this.

Cook got off to a bad start with his Private Office, and for that matter with the FCO generally, by not reading their papers. He likened himself to Ernest Bevin, who, he recounted, had made a joke about not reading five boxes his office had given him over the weekend. 'I'm happy to say', Cook declared ' that nobody's ever tried to present me with five red boxes, but ever since I heard that story I have recognized that you can be a successful Foreign Secretary if you focus on the big questions, not necessarily if you finish the paperwork.' This remark earned him two bad marks: he was boastful in comparing himself with Bevin; and it showed a disdain for the memos and drafts of the office. From his conduct in his early days in office it does not look as though Straw will be guilty of that sort of solecism. He is likely to get on well with his officials, even if on the diplomatic plane it will take him time to achieve the reputation his predecessor established with his ministerial colleagues in the European Union for pellucid and persuasive exposition.

Making up the box for overnight reading remains as delicate a task for the Private Secretary as it used to be in my time, depending not least on an understanding of the Secretary of State's predilections. Basically, the aim is to persuade him to get through it. Otherwise the work of the office is held up the following day. According to Douglas Hurd, who was Political Secretary to Edward Heath at No.10, the Prime Minister was tempted to get to the end of the box by the insertion of titbits about his yacht, *Morning Cloud*[19]. With Cook the lure was horses. So, interleaved with the heavy papers on how to prevent proliferation or about qualified voting in the EU Council of Ministers, warm invitations were inserted to go racing. Whether or not because of the Private Secretary's skilful exercise of this device, the fact is that no complaints came to be made later about Cook not getting through his paperwork. Needless to say, with Geoffrey Howe there was no problem in getting him to finish the box; the problem was to provide him with enough reading material to fill the many hours of the night when he did not want or need to sleep. For him it was a question of the more boxes the better.

When Alec Home was Foreign Secretary, boxes would be sent up to him in Ayrshire by the night train. Oliver Wright, his Principal Private Secretary, when invited to stay overnight, would tackle the boxes with Home before and after the day's shoot. They

---

19 Douglas, later Baron, Hurd, *An End to Promises*, Collins, 1979.

also met over picnic lunch when, as was said, they reviewed the cold war over the cold turkey.

The Private Secretary can exercise great influence over appointments, not simply because he is an *ex officio* member of the Senior Appointments Board, but on account of being the custodian of the Foreign Secretary's ear more consistently than any other member of the Diplomatic Service. Early in his time at the Foreign and Commonwealth Office Lord Carrington found himself embroiled in the issue of Rhodesia. Convinced that this subject deserved Rolls Royce attention, George Walden, his Principal Private Secretary, arranged for two members of the Service of the highest calibre, Robin Renwick and Charles Powell, to be given key responsibility for it. They made a decisive contribution to the outcome that was reached at the end of 1979[20]. Another example of the Private Secretary's opportunity to influence people's careers occurred over the appointment of the Head of the News Department, a post that amounts to being the Foreign Secretary's spokesman and is therefore of personal interest to him. It was Len Appleyard, then Private Secretary, who tipped off Geoffrey Howe about the particular qualities that would make Christopher Meyer ideal for the job. In 1984, he was accordingly given the appointment. This led to a glittering career in which Meyer later became successively Ambassador to Bonn and Washington.

Members of the Private Office have to maintain eternal vigilance in their relations with the office of the Permanent Under-Secretary of State. The general speeding up of communications and the intensification of direct dialogue between the Foreign

---

20 See *Lucky George,* George Walden, Penguin, 1998.

Secretary and his ministerial colleagues in the European Union have only enhanced this duty, just as more generally they have increased the responsibilities of the Private Office. The additional administrative load that the PUS[21] has to bear in modern conditions means that much depends on the Private Secretary to ensure that he is not kept out of the loop on policy issues. Yet the rapidity with which decisions often have to be reached may make this difficult. Brian Fall[22] has given me an example. The Foreign Secretary was summoned in great haste to No.10. He needed a brief. There was no time to secure anything from the Department so the Private Secretary, who knew the subject well, sketched out a note for him. Later, when the PUS heard about it, he was furious and reprimanded him. Why hadn't he been consulted before anything was put to the Minister in writing? The answer was obvious: no time. The Private Secretary knew that no harm had been done so far as policy was concerned, but he was tactful enough not to say so and to promise to be particularly careful in future. His destiny in the Service, he knew, would hang as much, perhaps more, on the PUS than on the Secretary of State; after all, the Private Secretary is blessed with a dual dependence as well as a dual loyalty.

The evolution of the European Union has compounded the responsibilities of the Private Secretary. The Foreign Secretary is constantly attending ministerial meetings with his European colleagues, or holding bilateral discussions with one Minister or another. He needs to have someone with him who knows the full

---

21 See Sir John Coles, *Making Foreign Policy: A Certain Idea of Britain,* John Murray, 2000.
22 Sir Brian Fall, Principal Private Secretary 1981–4.

sweep of the European agenda, and can provide the necessary advice as well as – and just as important – take a record. Nor can this be an official with wider responsibilities that preclude him from frequent absence abroad with the Secretary of State. The Private Secretary is the obvious person. But, in addition to the importance of his presence on the spot, he has to ensure that an account of the meeting is made available to all those who need to know – and these may be numerous, including ambassadors in posts abroad and ministers and officials at home, who may well be feeling left out. The Private Secretary will soon be made aware if he has omitted anyone who matters or if he has missed a trick or misled the minister. The episodes of Heseltine, Leon Brittan and the helicopters, and the Hinduja brothers have emphasized the need to ensure that records are kept of all ministerial talks, including those on the telephone.

During the Kosovo crisis the four leading European Foreign Secretaries (from the UK, Germany, France and Italy) and the US Secretary of State conducted a telephone conference at least once a week. Day-to-day responsibility for arranging such talks rested with the Private Secretary – another instance of the growing range of his obligations.

I cannot help thinking that the habitual reluctance of those in Private Offices to describe for public consumption the qualities of their masters may be a loss to history. Their close and uninterrupted observation can provide the opportunity for uniquely perceptive judgement. Douglas Hurd, later to become Foreign Secretary, only the second career diplomat ever to have done so, who was in Heath's Private Office at No.10 as Political Secretary, has shown a side of the Prime Minister scarcely visible to the public: 'Most elusive, and perhaps most difficult for others to believe was the wit, which was carefully concealed from the rest of the world, but was an essential part of his method of working. It did not take the form of verbal fireworks, let alone a string of jokes. The outrageous statement in a deadpan voice, the sardonic question, the long, quizzical silence ... It marked an approach to life – tough, humorous, impatient of empty phrases[23]'. I do not know a better picture than this of Heath, as he appeared to those who worked alongside him.

From personal experience I know how some ministers in the Wilson Governments of the sixties were troubled about being ruled or over-ruled by their officials, or at any rate were worried that others would suspect this. I have the impression that this is less so nowadays. This is because fewer of them have a complex about 'them and us'. They would be less inclined to say, as a senior Minister protested to me in the sixties, that Foreign Office officials saw things, not objectively from the standpoint of British interests, but from a one-sided frame of reference.

I continue to believe that on the whole officials want to be led rather than to lead. Jim Callaghan, however, has told me of prominent exceptions. At the FCO he was conscious of the confident self-assertiveness of FCO officials, compared with the self-effacing reticence of home civil servants. An example of this – searing to him perhaps at the time – was the strong pro-European bias of FCO officials in their briefing in the mid-sixties. He attributes this mettlesome spirit to the length of time FCO officials spend abroad, where they acquire, in Callaghan's description, a

---

23 Douglas Hurd, *An End to Promises*, Collins, 1979, p.137.

'semi-independence'. They are on their own. They have to be self-reliant. I believe another influence is at work. An official in a home department will be operating in the same field as his minister, whereas a diplomat abroad may well think that there is a good deal of local background that he knows about but that cannot be so evident to the minister. When he gets to serve at home this sense of superior knowledge and self-assurance is not readily sloughed off.

I have been eager to find out from present day private secretaries with whom I have spoken whether they share the prevailing scepticism of the public about politicians. Their response to my enquiries reflects, of course, their greater awareness, compared with those outside, of the heavy and often conflicting pressures upon those in public life, particularly from the media. They also clearly think it impossible to generalize, whether about their characters or their motives. They have led me to think that they would agree with Gladstone's hesitation: he always held that politicians were the men whom, as a rule, it was most difficult to comprehend. He declared that he had never understood, or thought he understood, above one or two. Disraeli was less puzzled. He was sure that real statesmen were inspired by nothing else than instinct for power and love of country.

When I first wrote on this subject in *The Private Office* the quality I picked out as paramount in politicians was love of the limelight. For them this translates itself into unremitting concern about the media. To no other body of men can the term love–hate be so pertinently applied as to politicians in their relationship with the Press. It will inevitably be part of the private secretary's job to try to get his master to treat with Kiplingesque indifference headlines of triumph and disaster. But he must not forget that, unlike him, the Minister depends on the buoyancy of votes, for which media publicity is the indispensable yeast.

I do not think I then did sufficient justice to the ceaseless longing of politicians for reassurance and devotion. They may get this at home, but it won't be enough. They need it from those who know at first hand the tensions and problems they have to encounter and that they have overcome. The struggle is harder for them now than it was for earlier generations. This is partly on account of the unremitting attention of the media, but also because for many in public life today there is not the same foursquare backing of family, church, club or local and vocational institutions upon which their forebears could so unfailingly rely. The private secretary is able to put in perspective the personalized venom his master may have had to endure from the domestic press against the respect he can well have earned from his foreign ministerial colleagues about which little is reported home.

This heightened stress of political life does not appear to have reduced the numbers of those wishing to enter the profession. I don't think that this is only due to the lure of the limelight. While I do not discount the evident vanity and personal ambition that contribute to the widespread contempt in which politicians are held nowadays, I still believe, as I suggested in my earlier account, that a sense of public duty and a desire to serve are part of the make-up of many of them, and that it is these qualities that often impelled them initially to embark on what an earlier generation dignified, perhaps romantically, as 'The Endless Adventure'.[24]

---

24 See F. S. Oliver, *The Endless Adventure*, Macmillan, 1930–35.

The forces that attract people to politics are of course extremely varied and frequently mixed. They are often as personal as they are unpredictable. In explaining why he entered politics, John Major has written that his motives were complex. He longed to be involved in the decisions that would shape his own life and times. But being 'insufficiently educated to advise ministers, I decided early on to be a minister myself, and to harness others' learning to my native good sense'.[25] Few others in public life would be so honest or so modest.

In conclusion, the overall impression I have derived from those who, over the past two decades, have worked in or alongside the Private Office of the FCO is that it continues to play the crucial role in policy-making that I outlined earlier. Indeed, for the reasons I have explained, it is even more of a linchpin than ever. As for the close-up picture I painted of politicians, I think my successors in the Private Office, aware of the increasing strains under which people in political life are working, would be cautious in adding warts to them, while recognizing the low esteem in which the public generally hold them – just as indeed the public likewise have little respect for those in many of the other traditional institutions of the country.

---

25 Major, Ibid, p. 182.

APPENDIX

Prime Ministers

Winston Churchill	1940–45
Clement Attlee	1945–51
Winston Churchill	1951–55
Anthony Eden	1955–57
Harold Macmillan	1957–63
Alex Douglas-Home	1963–4
Harold Wilson	1974–6
James Callaghan	1976–9
Margaret Thatcher	1979–90
John Major	1990–97
Tony Blair	1997– present

Foreign Secretaries

Anthony Eden	1940–45
Ernest Bevin	1945–51
Herbert Morrison	1951
Anthony Eden	1951–55

Harold Macmillan	1955
Selwyn Lloyd	1955–60
Alec Douglas-Home	1960–63
R. A. Butler	1963–4
Patrick Gordon Walker	1964–5
Michael Stewart	1965–6
George Brown	1966–8
Michael Stewart	1968–70
Alec Douglas-Home	1970–74
James Callaghan	1974–6
Tony Crosland	1976–7
David Owen	1977–9
Peter Carrington	1979–82
Francis Pym	1982–3
Geoffrey Howe	1983–9
John Major	1989
Douglas Hurd	1989–95
Malcolm Rifkind	1995–7
Robin Cook	1997–2001
Jack Straw	2001– present

BOOKS QUOTED

Attlee, C. R. *As It Happened*, Heinemann, 1954

Barclay, Sir Roderick, *Ernest Bevin and the Foreign Office*, Sir
  Roderick Barclay, 1975

Bullock, Alan, *Ernest Bevin*, Vol III (1954–51), Heinemann, 1983

Cadogan, *The Diaries of Sir Alexander, 1938–45*, (ed. David
  Dilks), Cassell, 1971

Churchill, Winston S., *The Second World War*, Cassell, 1954

Cole, John, *Making Foreign Policy: A Certain Idea of Britain*, John
  Murray, 2000

Cradock, Percy, *In Pursuits of British Interests*, John Murray, 1997

Crossman, R. H. S., *The Inside View*, Cape, 1972

Dalton, Hugh, *High Tide and After*, Muller, 1962

Dickie, John, *Inside the Foreign Office*, Chapmans, 1992

Dixon, Piers, *Double Diploma*, Hutchinson, 1968

Eden, Anthony, *Memoirs: The Reckoning*, Cassell, 1965

Hamilton, Mary Agnes, *Arthur Henderson: A Biography*,
  Heinemann, 1938

Harris, Kenneth, *David Owen*, Weidenfeld & Nicolson, 1987

Hennessy, Peter, *The Prime Minister*, Penguin, 2000
Hoare, Samuel, *Nine Troubled Years*, Collins, 1954
Howe, Geoffrey, *Conflict of Loyalty*, Macmillan, 1994
Hurd, Douglas, *An End to Promises*, Collins, 1979
Jones, Thomas, *A Diary with Letters*, OUP, 1938
Major, John, *The Autobiography*, HarperCollins, 1999
Nicolson, Harold, *Diaries and Letters 1939–45*, Collins, 1967
Oliver, F. S., *The Endless Adventure*, Macmillan 1930–35
Owen, David, *Time to Declare*, Michael Joseph, 1991
Petrie, Charles, *The Powers Behind the Prime Minister*,
    MacGibbon & Kee, 1938
Ponsonby, Charles, *Ponsonby Remembers*, The Alden Press, 1965
Rawnsley, Andrew, *Servants of the People*, Hamish Hamilton,
    2000
Stewart, Michael, *Life and Labour*, Sidgwick and Jackson, 1980
Strang, William, *The Foreign Office*, Allen & Unwin, 1955
Walden, George, *Lucky George*, Allen Lane, 1999

INDEX

Index